AF256385

AMERICA

ONE MILE AT A TIME for 15,828 MILES

BY

RICHARD IVES

This book is a work of non-fiction. Names and places have been changed to protect the privacy of all individuals. The events and situations are true.

© 2003 by Richard Ives. All rights reserved.

No part of this book may be reproduced, stored in a retrieval system, or transmitted by any means, electronic, mechanical, photocopying, recording, or otherwise, without written permission from the author.

ISBN: 1-4140-1292-6 (e-book)
ISBN: 1-4140-1291-8 (Paperback)

This book is printed on acid free paper.

1stBooks - rev. 10/08/03

CHAPTER 1

I WAS THIRTEEN YEARS OLD WHEN I REALLY NOTICED MY FIRST AMERICAN FLAG. SURE, I HAD PLACED MY HAND ON MY HEART BEFORE CLASS EACH MORNING AT SCHOOL AND RECITED THE PLEDGE OF ALLEGIANCE WHILE STARING AT THE SAME FLAG, AND YES I HAD EVEN SANG THE STAR SPANGLED BANNER BEFORE MY LITTLE LEAGUE BASEBALL GAMES—BUT, ON NOVEMBER 1963, WHEN I SAW ON TV, THE AMERICAN FLAG DRAPPED OVER JOHN F. KENNEDY'S COFFIN, I REMEMBER THE SORROW AROUND ME. AT THAT SAME MOMENT MY MOTHER WAS STANDING AT THE IRONING BOARD WATCHING THE T.V. WITH ME, SHE JOINED IN WITH THE WHOLE COUNTRY TO SHED TEARS. FROM THAT DAY FORWARD I HAD A DESIRE TO SEE AND LEARN MORE ABOUT AMERICA. A DREAM TO TRAVEL! A DREAM TO SEE!! A DREAM TO SHARE!!!!

SOMEWHERE AROUND 15 I STARTED COLLECTING MAPS AND DRAWING DIFFERENT ROUTES THAT WOULD GIVE ME THE BEST LOOK AT AMERICA. HIDEING MY DREAM AND CONTINUOUSLY BUILDING ON IT WAS MY SECRET. A LITTLE BOY DEVELOPING INTO A MAN HAS IT'S MOMENTS; THOSE MOMENTS COULD BE STRETCHED INTO HIS DREAMS. I REMEMBER THESE MOMENTS VERY VIVIDLY BECAUSE I WAS ALWAYS WANTING TO CATCH UP TO A BROTHER THAT WAS ONE YEAR OLDER AND TO ME- WHAT I WANTED TO BE. BUT…THAT'S ANOTHER STORY…MY DREAM TO VISIT AMERICA STARTED TO TAKE SHAPE WHEN MY FATHER BOUGHT A SEARS AND

ROEBUCKS RED ALLSTATE CUSHMAN SCOOTER. WE'RE TALKING ABOUT A 25 HP, RED BOX WITH WHEELS THAT WOULD MAYBE REACH 45—48 MPH DOWNHILL. A LAWNMOWER ENGINE AND A WATERMELLON SHAPED GAS TANK AND WHAT LOOKED LIKE A SWINN BICYCLE HANDLE. THE DAMN THING WAS UGLY BUT WE DIDN'T HAVE TO PEDDLE!!!

BEING OLDER MY BROTHER DROVE ME EVERYWHERE FOR MONTHS. I JUST HAD TO FIND A WAY TO GET IN CONTROL! THEN IT HAPPENED. A FRIEND OF MINE GOT SICK AND HE ASK ME TO THROW HIS PAPERS FOR HIM. MY FIRST "BIKE" WAS FINALLY IN FIRM GRIP. YOU KNOW THAT FEELING IF YOU EVER HAD A BIKE. I'M NOT TALKING ABOUT OWNING OR RIDING OR HAVING A BIKE—I'M TALKING ABOUT GRIPPING YOUR BIKE. YOU KNOW— IT'S YOURS, NO ONE ELSES', WHEN YOU MOVE IT MOVES, WHEN IT PURRS YOU PURR AND EVERYONE KNOWS IT'S A PART OF YOU. I LEARNED LATER IN LIFE THAT THIS SAME TYPE OF FEELING ABOUT MY BIKE COULD BE SHARED WITH MY COUNTRY. THIS, BY THE WAY, IS THE MOST COMMON THREAD TO MOTORCYCLE RIDERS—THE LOVE OF THEIR COUNTRY.

NOW THAT I HAD A BIKE THE MAPS I HAD COLLECTED BECAME EVEN MORE INTERESTING TO ME. SECRETLY WHEN MY BROTHER AND SISTERS WERE WATCHING TV OR TALKING ABOUT DIFFERENT PLACES I WOULD INSTANTLY SEE MYSELF ON A BIKE AT THAT SAME PLACE. YOU REMEMBER THOSE MOMENTS WHEN THE TEACHER CAUGHT YOU DAY DREAMING OR

WHEN IT WAS RAINING AND THE BUBBLES IN THE ROAD WOULD PUT YOU IN

A TRANCE—MY MOMENTS WERE ALWAYS ON A BIKE OF COURSE ABOUT

THAT TIME MY BROTHER WOULD COME BY AND SMACK ME UP SIDE THE

HEAD AND MY DREAM WOULD BE INTERRUPTED BY ONE OF OUR MANY

BRAWLS—MY FATHER SAID IT WAS JUST PART OF BEING BOYS—BUT THAT'S

ANOTHER STORY…

THE DREAM WAS GETTING CLOSER WHEN "PETER FONDA" CAME RACING

ACROSS THE SCREEN AND WE WERE ALL LETTING OUR HAIR GROW OUT.

I DIDN'T PARTICULARLY LIKE THE ENDING TO THE MOVIE BUT HIS "BIKE"

LIVES ON. "CAPTAIN AMERICA BIKES" ARE COPIED AND ROAD ALL OVER

OUR COUNTRY. IT'S A COMMON BIKE AT LOCAL RUNS. NEXT TIME YOU SEE

ONE NOTICE HOW MANY PEOPLE ARE LOOKING AT IT. I GUARANTEE YOU

THEY ARE LOOKING AT MORE THAN THE BIKE. THAT CHOPPER WITH THE

AMERICAN FLAG ON THE GAS TANK CAN CAUSE A LOT OF MINDS TO GO

BACK OR FORWARD. MINE WENT FORWARD. I WAS NOW DOWN TO MAKING

A LIST OF ITEMS TO TAKE ON MY TRIP WITH ME. LET'S SEE: 4 PAIRS OF

SOCKS, 4 PAIR OF UNDERWARE, FIELD JACKET, LEATHERS, GLOVES…BUT—

YET ANOTHER INTERRUPTION!! I WAS DRAFTED.

THERE I WAS AGAIN, STANDING INFRONT OF THE AMERICAN FLAG WITH

MY HAND ON MY HEART. I KNEW I WAS HEADED TO VIET NAM BUT I COULD

ONLY SEE MY DREAMS BETWEEN THE RED AND WHITE STRIPES. MY DREAM

OF BEING ON THE ROAD GOT ME THROUGH THE NEXT TWO YEARS AND I

BROKE SILENCE OF MY DREAM ONE NIGHT TO A FRIEND. WHAT HAD BEEN ALMOST SACRED TO ME AND SO CLOSE TO MY INTERMOST FEELING WAS NOW OUT IN THE OPEN. I WAS NOT SURPRISED WHEN JACK ACTED UNINTERRESTED, IT WAS EVEN SOMEWHAT OF A RELIEF. FOR NOW, IT MIGHT BECOME MY SECRET AGAIN! WEEKS BEFORE HE GOT OUT OF THE ARMY HE GAVE ME HIS ADDRESS AND ASK ME TO SEND A COPY OF THE TRIP TO HIM. YEAH RIGHT, HOW MANY TIMES DO FRIENDS POLITELY ACT INTERESTED BECAUSE THEY ARE YOUR FRIENDS ONLY TO POLITELY EXCUSE THEMSELVES LATER ON. NOT TO DISCOURAGE MYSELF I BLEW IT OFF AND CONTINUED TO PLAN MY TRIP WHICH WAS NOW DOWN TO DAILY STOPS AT WHAT NATIONAL PARK ON WHAT DAY. TALK ABOUT A GUY THAT WAS HOOKED ON AN IDEA.

TWO MONTHS BEFORE I GOT OUT OF THE ARMY I HITCHHIKED HOME TO EL PASO, TEXAS ON A WEEKEND PASS. ANOTHER DELAY OF MY TRIP WAS ABOUT TO HAPPEN AND I DIDN'T KNOW IT. A GIRLFRIEND (NOW MY WIFE OF 30 YEARS) HAD JUST COME BACK TO EL PASO. WE HAD LOST TOUCH DURING THE PAST 2 YEARS. THIS WAS THE FIRST TIME THAT MY DREAM ACTUALLY WAS IN JEAPARDY. HER DREAM ON THE OTHER HAND WAS QUICKLY BEING INTRODUCED TO ME. (DON'T THROW THE BOOK AWAY GUYS THIS ISN'T GOING TO GET MUSHY)

WE BECAME ENGAGED WITH A PRE-NUPTUAL AGGREEMENT BEFORE IT BECAME POPULAR TO HAVE SUCH A THING. SHE, WAS TO QUIT SMOKING AND I, WAS TO GO ON MY "BIKE TRIP". SOUNDS ONE SIDED BUT FAIR TO ME!!!! ANYONE WANT TO VOTE?

WHEN I GOT BACK TO THE BARRACKS IN COLORADO SPRINGS A LETTER FROM JACK WAS WAITING FOR ME. TO MY SURPRISE HE HAD GONE DOWN MY LIST AND BOUGHT EACH ITEM. WHEN I LISTED ONE BLUE HONDA 350SL, HE BOUGHT ONE—NEXT ITEM, ONE 35mm CAMERA, HE BOUGHT ONE, 4 PAIRS OF SOCKS, HE'S GOT THEM…AND SO ON.

I WAS NUMB! I WAS LESS THAN 7 WEEKS AWAY FROM MY DREAM AND AFTER MANY SETBACKS AND DELAYS - - IT FELT, FOR THE FIRST TIME, IT MIGHT HAPPEN. I TOOK A BIG BREATH OF FRESH AIR, WHICH IS NOT HARD TO DO IN FORT CARSON, COLORADO - LOOKED OUT AT PIKES PEAK AND REALIZED THAT A FEW WEEKS FROM THEN I WOULD BE TRAVELING UP AND DOWN AND AROUND SCENIC SPOTS JUST LIKE THIS MOUNTAIN. COME ON NOW, JOIN WITH ME—SHUT YOUR EYES AND REMEMBER THAT ONE DREAM THAT HAUNTED YOU FOREVER THAT WAS ALWAYS JUST OUT OF REACH. THAT'S HOW I HAD ALWAYS FELT.

JACKS PLANS TO MEET ME AT THE GATE TO START OUR TRIP SENT CHILLS DOWN MY BACK. IT WAS PARTY TIME! BUT - THAT'S ANOTHER STORY…PUT THE BOOK DOWN AND GO GET A BEER OR JUST TAKE A SHORT BREAK BECAUSE YOU'RE ABOUT TO JOIN JACK AND I ON A COAST TO COAST, CANADA TO MEXICO BIKE TRIP WE WILL NEVER FORGET.

CHAPTER 2

AUGUST 10TH 1971—21 YEARS OLD, FRESH OUT OF THE ARMY, NO MORE

YES SIR—NO SIR. KATHY HAD GIVEN ME A GREEN LIGHT TO GET THE TRIP

OUT OF MY SYSTEM BEFORE WE TIED THE KNOT, AND JACK SHOWED!!! HE IS

ON THE RIGHT, A QUIET GUY, BUT ONE THAT YOU'RE COMFORTABLE

CALLING A FRIEND—YOU KNOW THE TYPE! HE DROVE ALL THE WAY FROM

FOND-DU-LAC, WISCONSIN TO MEET ME. I MUST HAVE SPARKED AN

INTEREST SOMEWHERE IN OUR EARLY CONVERSATIONS BECAUSE HE WAS

ALL SMILES AND READY TO RIDE. WE WERE NO HELL'S ANGELS (THEY MEET UP WITH US TWICE IN THIS BOOK) BUT WITH LEATHERS ON AND BOOTS SHINED OUR BUDDIES SAW US OFF WITH SEVERAL LARGE HERO SANDWICHES FROM THE MESS HALL. NOW YOU GUYS OUT THERE THAT SAY ARMY FOOD IS TERRIBLE YOU NEED TO OWN UP! I REMEMBER THE ICE COLD MILK, THE EVER PRESENT LUMPY MASHED POTATOES, THE S—ON THE SHINKLES—OH WELL, THAT'S ANOTHER STORY…

A TRADITIONAL HAND SHAKE AND A QUICK KICK TO START OUR HONDA 350SL'S AND AWAY WE GO. OH BY THE WAY, WHEN WE LEFT THE GATE WE WAVED GOODBY TO OUR BARRACKS PARTNERS THE "MP'S) THERE RESPONSE WAS THAT WE WERE EITHER #1 IN THEIR BOOKS OR…YOU GET THE PICTURE. THE WEATHER WAS GREAT AND NOTHING COULD STOP US NOW. WE BOLTED ONTO I-25 AND HEADED TOWARDS DENVER. HEY, WAIT A MINUTE! WHAT HAPPENED TO THE ATTRACTIONS AROUND COLORADO SPRINGS? WELL, LIKE ALL TRIPS YOU TAKE FROM HOME, YOUR NOT INTERESTED IN SEEING AGAIN WHAT YOU KNOW ABOUT. PLACES LIKE "GARDEN OF THE GODS", "SEVEN FALLS", "WILL ROGERS SHRINE OF THE SUN" ooh, AND DON'T FORGET "CRIPPLE CREEK" AND "THE ROYAL GORGE BRIDGE" AND…WELL YOU GET THE PICTURE. MY ADVICE IS NOT TO JUST PASS THROUGH THIS AREA. IF YOU HAVE THE TIME; PIKES PEAK BY ITSELF IS A GOOD HALF DAY OR FOR MANY A VERY REWARDING FULL DAY JORNEY.

WE JUST WANTED TO GET SOME MILES BETWEEN US AND HOME BASE QUICK! SO WE EVEN PASSED UP THE AIR FORCE ACADEMY AND THEN FOCUSED ON THE MOUNTAINS TO OUR LEFT. THE ROCKY MOUNTAIN NATIONAL PARK WAS TO BE OUR FIRST ITEM TO CHECK OFF OUR LIST. YOU KNOW "THE LIST." THE ONE I HAD BEEN MAKING NOTES ON FOR THE PAST UMPTEEN YEARS. THE PEN WAS IN MY HEAD AND I COULD NOT WAIT TO CHECK AN ITEM OFF. WE WERE IN A SELF SURVIVAL MODE AND CITY LIFE OR BUILDINGS WASN'T THE ANSWER.

JACK AND I HAD NOT RIDDEN WITH EACH OTHER MUCH YET AND WE WERE ALREADY DEVELOPING SIGNALS. HE OR I WOULD POINT AND WE WOULD GIVE THUMBS UP OR DOWN OR POINT FORWARD TO INDICATE LET'S KEEP RIDING. IT WAS A GLORIOUS DAY, THE SUN WAS PEAKING THROUGH THE CLOUDS AND A COOL AUGUST AIR WAS WELCOMED, IT JUST FIT THE SITUATION. WITH OUR HELMETS SHIELDS DOWN, IT WAS DIFFICULT TO CATCH THE OTHERS EMOTIONS, BUT, JUST LIKE A PERSONS BODY LANGUAGE YOU CAN TELL A PERSONS RIDING LANGUAGE; AT LEAST MINE ANYWAY! JACK WAS USUALLY ALL SERIOUS AND TASK ORIENTED (NOW IN THE COMPUTER PROGRAMING INDUSTRY) I ON THE OTHER HAND WAS WEAVING BETWEEN THE STRIPS AND MAKING HAND JESTURES AND DANCING TO THE MUSIC IN MY HEAD (I ENDED UP IN SALES) I'M SURE, IN FACT I WOULD BET ON IT, HE'S SMARTER BUT I CAN ENCOURAGE FUN. (ANOTHER WAY OF SAYING I CAN GET INTO TROUBLE) TAKE ANOTHER SIP OF YOUR BEER OR WHATEVER AND COME ON—LET'S HAVE SOME FUN.

THIS WAS, AS SOME OF YOU REMEMBER, A VERY VOLATILE TIME IN OUR COUNTRY; WITH THE VIET NAM WAR GOING ON AND ALL THE RIOTS AND FLOWER CHILDREN LETTING THEIR HAIR DOWN. IT WAS EASY FOR ME TO SWITCH OVER TO THE OTHER SIDE IN AN INSTANCE. IN DENVER I HAD NO PROBLEM PULLING UP TO A CONVERTIBLE WITH 3 GIRLS IN IT AND ASKING FOR DIRECTIONS. HELL, I HAD BEEN MAPING THIS TRIP FOREVER I KNEW WERE I WAS AND I KNEW WERE I WAS GOING. JACK AT TIMES WANDERED IF I HAD ANYTHING BETWEEN MY EARS BUT HE HUMORED ME ANYWAY. WELL, WE STOPPED FOR GAS IN DENVER AND MADE A QUICK ENTRY IN OUR LOGS (MILES DRIVEN, 70 CENTS FOR GAS, LOCATION AND ANY QUICK NOTES). TALLY HO AND AWAY WE GO—

<u>COLORADO ROCKY MOUNTAIN NATIONAL PARK</u>

AS THE PHOTO SUGGEST WE HIT THE PARK ENTRANCE LATER IN THE AFTERNOON AND THE CLOUD COVER WAS SHADOWING THE SCENERY. THE RAINBOW CURVE ROADSIDE INFORMATIONAL SIGN IS TYPICAL OF MANY, MANY, MANY WE WOULD STOP AND READ AND GIVE OURSELVES A BREAK.

IT WAS OUR FIRST DAY OF 53 AND THE FIELD JACKETS CAME OUT. THE
SNOW TOPPED MOUNTAINS AND TREES OFFERED SMELLS AND PRESTINE
COLORS THAT CAN NOT BE EQUALED WITH WORDS. THE EXPERIENCE FROM
THE SEAT OF A MOTORCYCLE JUST MAGNIFIES THESE SENCES THAT ONE
TAKES FOR GRANTED. YOU'VE BEEN THERE! LIKE WHEN YOU PASS BY A
BAKERY AND SMELL FRESH BREAD, OR TASTE YOUR FAVORITE DESSERT.
JACK AND I WERE STANDING AT THE SIGN AND SMELLING NATURE IN ALL
HER GLORY, LISTENING TO THE BREEZE AND SMALL ANIMALS, FEELING THE
MOISTNESS IN THE AIR AND LOOKING OUT AT EVERYTHING - - JUST
SOAKING IT IN. OH YEAH, WHAT ABOUT TASTE!? WELL, WE ATE A
SANDWICH!

AFTER LOTS OF PHOTOS WE WERE ABOUT TO EXPERIENCE OUR FIRST
NIGHT. THE SUN WENT DOWN AND WE FOUND OURSELVES IN A VERY
SMALL TOWN OF LAKELAND, COLORADO. STOPPED AT A GAS STATION, THE
ATTENDANT WAS CLOSING DOWN BUT HELPED US ANYWAY. HE (OR WE)
WERE QUICKLY REWARDED BECAUSE A VW VAN PULLED UP AND TWO
GIRLS GOT OUT LOOKING LIKE THEY JUST CAME FROM WOODSTOCK. I CAN
SHUT MY EYES AND SEE IT TODAY. BOTH WERE ABOUT 19 WITH LIGHT HAIR,
BELL BOTTOMS, LOSE TOPS WITH LACY FRAYED SLEEVES AND FLOWERS
PAINTED IN DIFFERENT PLACES, BUT EYE CATCHING PLACES, IF YOU KNOW
WHAT I MEAN. JACK AND I WAS IN FOR A SURPRISE. THE ATTENDANT
OFFERED HIS TRAILER TO ALL OF US FOR THE NIGHT AND A PARTY
STARTED. NOW, NOWHERE, I MEAN NOWHERE IN MY PLANS OR DREAMS DID

I EVER WRITE THIS INTO MY TRIP—YET AS QUIET AND STRAIGHTFORWARD

OF A GUY JACK IS—I DON'T RECALL ANY COMPLAINTS.

ON MY FIELD JACKET MY AMERICAN FLAG WITH A PEACE SIGN ON IT

TOOK ON A WHOLE NEW MEANING. COME TO THINK ABOUT IT THE 5 SENSES

I WAS JUST BRAGING ABOUT WERE FINE TUNED ONCE AGAIN.

WOW—WHAT A WAY TO START A TRIP! WE HAD STARTED ONE MORE

ITEM THAT WAS NOT ON MY LIST—EACH NIGHT FROM THEN ON WE WOULD

BUY A "DIFFERENT BRAND OR FLAVOR" OF BEER TO END THE EVENING.

THERE IS SOME BAD BEER OUT THERE - BUT THAT'S ANOTHER STORY…

DAY 2—AUGUST 11TH, 1971—WEDNESDAY

THE NEXT MORNING WE HAD TO PINCH OURSELVES AND DECIDE: TO STAY OR TO GO? DECISIONS, DECISIONS, DECISIONS. WE WENT! STEAMBOAT SPRINGS WAS OUR NEXT GAS STOP ON THE WAY TO **DINOSAUR NATIONAL PARK**.

THE EXPERIENCE OF DRIVING THROUGHVERY DIFFERENT AREAS IN THE SAME DAY HAS A TENDANCY TO SHARPEN BOTH ENDS OF THE SPECTRUM. BOTH AREAS WERE EQUALLY BEAUTIFUL BUT ALSO HAD SHARP CONTRAST. ONE HAD TALL TREES AND LUSH GREEN COLORS, THE OTHER HAD SMALL SHUBS AND DULL BROWN COLORS! EACH AREA HAD IT'S VISITOR CENTERS WHICH WE ALWAYS TOOK ADVANTAGE OF AND THE PARKS WERE ALWAYS KEPT CLEAN BUT THAT'S WHERE THE SIMULARITIES ENDED. LOOK CLOSE AND YOU CAN SEE THE DUSTY DIRT ROAD WE TOOK. THAT WAS PROBABLY THE REASON FOR OUR NEXT SPONTANIOUS ADVENTURE.

SORRY GIRLS AND I KNOW YOU GUYS APPRECIATED ME CUTTING THE BOTTOM OF THE PICTURE OFF! YEP! IT WAS TIME FOR A SHOWER. WE WERE JUST CASUALLY RUNNING DOWN THE ROAD WHEN I BREAKED HARD AND JACK KEPT GOING. HE RETURNED ONLY TO FIND ME WITH A S—EATING GRIN AND A WILD IDEA. IT SEEMS AN IRRIGATION DITCH HAD SPRUNG A LEAK AND WALLA! IT'S SHOWER TIME. WE HAD NO IDEA HOW FORTUNATE WE WERE THEN COMPARED TO THE REST OF OUR TRIP. EVERYTHING WAS GOING RIGHT. NOTICE JACK'S NICE SHORTS, AFTER TWO YEARS OF SHOWERING WITH HALF THE ARMY HE'S HESITANT TO SHOW JOE PUBLIC WHAT NATURE GAVE HIM.

OKAY—CLEANED, WIDE AWAKE AND JACK SCARED OF WHAT I'M GOING TO DO NEXT - WE GET BACK ON OUR TRUSTY STEEDS (I'M FROM TEXAS BY THE WAY). WE POINT OUR BIKES SOUTH TOWARDS GRAND JUNCTION, COLORADO. HEY, IF YOU HAVEN'T GOT A MAP OUT YET YOUR MISSING HALF THE FUN. I'LL PAUSE WHILE YOU GO GET ONE.

OKAY NOW—AS YOU NOTICED WE'RE COVERING SOME MILES HERE. WE HAVE OUR SIGHTS ON "**<u>COLORADO NATIONAL MONUMENT</u>**" AND AT AN AVERAGE OF 55 MPH (HEY IT'S A 350 HONDA) WE'LL MAKE IT.

AFTER GASING UP IN GRAND JUNCTION (75 CENTS AND MY LOG SAYS A COKE - 10 CENTS) WE LOOKED SOUTH OF THE CITY AND COULD SEE WHERE WE WERE GOING. THE PICTURES EVEN SHOW THE CITY LIGHTS IN THE DISTANCE!

WE SAVED ANOTHER TWO BUCKS AT THE ENTRANCE DUE TO JACK SUGGESTING EACH OF US PURCHASE A "GOLDEN EAGLE PARK PASS" BEFORE THE TRIP. HE'S SO SMART! INDEPENDENCE MONUMENT AT THE PARK HAS EVEN HAD A WEDDING PERFORMED ON IT'S PENTICAL PEAK! JACK THOUGHT THAT WAS COOL, HELL, I WAS WAITING FOR THE NEXT SIX-PACK.

ASK AND YOU SHALL RECEIVE—IT WAS GETTING DARK AND WE FOUND A ROAD SIDE PARK AND THREW OUR SLEEPING BAGS OUT, SAT DOWN, DRANK SOME SUDS, AND JOTTED NOTES IN OUR JOURNALS. MY CONVERSATION MUST HAVE BEEN BORING BECAUSE I LOOKED OVER AND JACK WAS ASLEEP. (SO I DRANK HIS BEER)

DAY 3—AUGUST 12TH, 1971—THURSDAY

NOW—I DON'T KNOW IF IT WAS THE EXTRA BEER OR THAT JACK WAS EXTRA TIRED (OR MAYBE BOTH). BUT, WE BOTH SLEPT PAST SUNRISE, AND THAT'S BAD. YOU SEE, WHEN THE SUN COMES UP THE CREATURES OF THIS WORLD START STIRING. IT DOESN'T MATTER WHO YELLED FIRST, BUT YELL WE DID. IT SEEMS WE HAD THROWN OUR BAGS RIGHT ON TOP OF SEVERAL, I'M SAYING MANY, ANT HOLES. HE LOOKED AT ME AND I LOOKED AT HIM AND LAUGHED (ONLY FOR A SECOND) AND IT WAS ALL ABOUT WHO COULD TAKE HIS CLOTHS OFF FIRST. WE MUST HAVE BEEN QUITE AN ATTRACTION FOR GRANDMA TRAVELING WITH FAMILY WHO JUST HAPPENED TO BE PARKED A HUNDRED YARDS AWAY. WE WERE BOTH STILL HALF ASLEEP AND WIDE AWAKE AT THE SAME TIME. BUT—THAT'S ANOTHER STORY…

BACK ON THE BIKES; WE BOTH HAD HEARD ABOUT **<u>ARCHES NATIONAL PARK</u>** MANY TIMES IN OUR LIVES. ROAD RUNNER - COYOTE CARTOONS, TV SHOWS ECT. NOTHING THAT WE HEARD DID IT JUSTICE! BUT WHAT WE SEE ON CARTOONS IS CLOSE. BELIEVE IT! THOSE WEIRD ROCK FORMATIONS ARE THERE. OKAY, DON'T BELIEVE ME, SEE THE PICTURES.

I TOOK OVER 15 PICTURES AND THEY ALL HAVE WEIRD FORMATIONS IN

THEM. (ONE OF THEM WAS JACK). THE PARK HAS A LOOP ROAD AND IT

MADE THE SAME IMPRESSION ON BOTH OF US. WE BOTH SAW DIFFERENT

AND JUST AS ODD/BEAUTIFUL FORMATIONS ON THE WAY OUT AS WE DID ON

THE WAY IN. THAT MEANS THAT SOME DAY JACK AND I WILL HAVE TO TAKE

THE WHOLE TRIP AGAIN BACKWARDS. (BUT NOT ON 350'S)

THE NEXT COUPLE OF STOPS REALLY PEAKED JACK'S INTEREST BECAUSE

HE IS FROM THE EAST AND WAS VERY UNFAMILIAR WITH THE SOUTHWEST.

IT GAVE ME THE OPPORTUNITY TO SHARE THOSE THINGS I KNEW ABOUT

THE DESERT.

<u>MESA VERDE NATIONAL PARK</u> SHOWED US EXAMPLES OF HOW THE INDIANS LIVED IN THIS AREA YEARS AGO. IT IS A REAL EYE OPENER TO WALK AMONG THESE DWELLINGS. THE SITES HAVE BEEN PRESERVED TO THE POINT THAT IT IS NOT DIFFICULT TO IMAGINE THE LIFE STYLE AND ACTIVITIES OF THE AREA.

FOUR CORNERS WAS A SMALL DISTANCE FROM WHERE WE WERE, SO, A BEER AND A LIMB IN EACH STATE SOUNDED LIKE A WAY TO END THE DAY. WHEN WE GOT THERE, TO OUR SURPRISE IT WASN'T MUCH OF ANYTHING. I DON'T REALLY KNOW WHAT WE EXPECTED, BUT A CONCRETE SLAB WITH AN "X "IN IT WASN'T FULLFILLING. BUT, THE BEER WAS. NIGHT, NIGHT!

DAY 4—AUGUST 13TH, 1971—FRIDAY

HERE WE GO! DAY 4—AND EVEN THOUGH IT WAS "FRIDAY THE 13TH" WE WOKE UP WITH OUR SCALPS INTACT. JACK SAYS INDIANS DON'T DO THAT ANYMORE, BUT WHAT DO EASTERNERS KNOW ANYWAY! THE NEXT FEW STOPS ALL CENTERED AROUND INDIAN RUINS; **<u>AZTEC RUINS NATIONAL PARK, CHACO CANYON, EL MORO NATIONAL MONUMENT</u>**.

EACH HAD THERE DISTINCT ARCHITECTURE AND HISTORY WHICH PEOPLE MISS IF THEY DON'T TAKE IN THE VISITOR CENTERS. BESIDES - THESE CENTERS ALL HAVE RESTROOMS. I WAS GETTING RESTLESS AND I HADN'T SCARED ANYONE LATELY SO TO PASS TIME ON THE ROAD I WAS MESSING AROUND. WE HAD BEEN PASSING THROUGH SHORT CLOUD BURST

ALL AFTERNOON WHEN COMING AROUND A CORNER IN GRANTS, N.M. JACK DROPPED HIS BIKE. I SWEAR I WASN'T ANYWHERE NEAR HIM. I BELIEVE HE HIT A SANDY PART OF THE ROAD COMING AROUND THE CORNER AND JUST LOST IT. HE WAS ONLY DOING ABOUT 5 MPH SO THE ONLY THING THAT GOT HURT WAS HIS PRIDE. I DID STOP HORSING AROUND THOUGH—WELL, FOR AT LEAST 10 MINUTES OR SO. FRIDAY THE 13TH AND ALL, WE WERE BOTH GLAD WE GOT THROUGH WITH NO MAJOR CATASTROPHIES. BESIDES, TOMORROW IS ANOTHER DAY.

DAY 5—AUGUST 14TH, 1971—SATURDAY

SATURDAY WAS NO PIC-NIC! FIRST OF ALL WE WOKE UP AT ANOTHER ROADSIDE PARK, BUT THIS TIME TWO GUYS WHO WERE UGLIER THAN JACK HAD CURLED UP NEXT TO US. NOW, COUNT BACK AT HOW MANY DAYS SINCE OUR LAST SHOWER. THREE - RIGHT! WELL, WE WERE RIPE, BUT THESE GUYS WERE RIPER. I THINK IF GIVEN A CHOICE WE WOULD HAVE PICKED THE ANT BEDS AGAIN. JACK AND I FIGURED OUT THAT IT'S NOT GOOD THAT BOTH OF US WERE SOUND SLEEPERS! SO QUICKLY, WITHOUT EXCHANGING PHONE NUMBERS WE WERE ON OUR WAY TO—

WHITE SANDS, NEW MEXICO: THE SUN WAS HOT AND THE SAND WAS HOTTER. IF YOU'VE NEVER BEEN, PICTURE A BEACH AND THEN BLEACH IT WHITER THAN WHITE AND TAKE AWAY ALL SIGNS OF LIFE. THAT'S NOTTRUE ACCORDING TO THE VISITORS CENTER BUT THAT'S HOW JACK FELT. I ON THE OTHER HAND LIVED IN EL PASO, TEXAS MOST OF MY LIFE AND THIS SPOT WAS A FAVORITE WEEKEND TRIP. SAND SURFING, SAND FOOTBALL…SAND SPORTS PERIOD WAS ENOUGH TO KEEP THIS NATIONAL MONUMENT BUSY. WELL, OUR LEATHERS WERE STARTING TO STICK TO OUR BODIES SO IT WAS TIME TO ROLL! COMING OUT OF THE PARK WE KNEW WE WERE ONLY A 100 MILES OR SO TO A BATH AND FRESH SHEETS. WE ALSO NOTED SEVERAL LARGE CLOUDS THAT WERE GETTING DARKER. WELL, AS

RICHARD IVES

LUCK HAS IT ONE CAUGHT US ONLY 15 MILES FROM EL PASO. WE DID THE UNTHINKABLE FOR SOMEONE WHO KNEW THE SOUTHWEST. WHEN IT STARTED HITTING US, JACK STOPPED AND STARTED PUTTING ON HIS RAINGEAR. I SHOULD HAVE GONE ON, BUT I STOPPED AND DID THE SAME. ONE MILE DOWN THE ROAD IT WAS CLEAR AGAIN. THAT'S COMMON IN THE SOUTHWEST DURING THE AFTERNOON. A SINGLE CLOUD WILL DEVELOP A CELL AND WORK BY ITSELF. ANYWAY THE PHOTO SPEAKS FOR ITSELF.

LIKE SOAKED ALLEY CATS WE ARRIVED IN EL PASO, TEXAS.

<u>CHAPTER 3</u>

DAY 6 & 7 WAS SPENT CLEANING UP AND REPAIRING THE BIKES. I TOOK

A LINK OUT OF MY CHAIN AND WELDED THE SISSY BAR UP. THERE WERE

PARTIES AND VISITS TO JUAREZ, MEXICO AND THEN THERE WAS

KATHY…WELL, THAT'S ANOTHER STORY…

DAY 8—AUGUST 17TH, 1971—TUESDAY

I WAS ASKED "WHEN WILL YOU BE BACK"? WE HAD NO WAY OF

KNOWING THE NUMBER OF DAYS BECAUSE I NEVER PUT A TIME LIMIT ON

THE TRIP. WE WENT WHERE WE WANTED AND STAYED AS LONG AS NEEDED

TO CAPTURE THE DIFFERENT LOOKS, SMELLS, AND FEELINGS OF THE AREA.

BY THE TIME WE GOT CLOSE TO OUR NEXT SCHEDULED STOP (TOMBSTONE,

ARIZONA) WE HAD BEEN RIDING IN THE RAIN FOR AN HOUR. SINCE WE SAW

THIS AS JUST ANOTHER TOWN WE PRESSED ON TOTUCSON. THE HEAT,

HUMIDITY, RAIN, MUD PUDDLES AND 1 HOUR RAIN DELAY AT A FILLING

STATION SET THE TONE FOR THE REST OF THE TRIP. ON A MOTORCYCLE, THE

RAIN CAN WEAR YOU DOWN. THAT'S WHY WE TRIED TO CHECK INTO A

YMCA IN PHOENIX. SHOWERS WERE $2.50 AND TO SLEEP ANOTHER $4.00.

OUR BUDGET COULDN'T TAKE THAT SO ANOTHER ROAD SIDE PARK WAS

HOME FOR THE NIGHT. WE DIDN'T REALLY APPRECIATE IT THAT MUCH IN

THE DARK.

23

DAY 9—AUGUST 18TH, 1971—WEDNESDAY

WE WOKE UP EARLY THE NEXT MORNING AND THIS SITE TURNED OUT TO BE A VERY GOOD CHOICE. THE FACILITIES WERE NEW AND I CAN'T IMAGINE THE YMCA BEING TOO MUCH BETTER. WE HAD A ROOF OVER OUR HEADS, A PLACE TO TAKE A SPONGE BATH AND THE WHOLE SKY AS OUR LIVINGROOM!

CHECK YOUR MAP OUT, WE THEN STOPPED AT **MONTEZUMA CASTLE**, **TZIGOOT**, **WALNUT CANYON**, **SUNSET CRATER** AND **WUPATKI NATIONAL MONUMENTS**. A BIG DAY FOR INDIAN RUINS AND SOUTHWEST STYLE DWELLINGS. THE SKY WAS CLEAR AND TRAVELING TIME BETWEEN SITES WAS MINIMAL. TODAY WAS MORE SITE SEEING THAN RIDING.

EACH SITE HAD IT'S OWN STORY TO TELL. THESE PICTURES ARE BUT A FEW OF MANY WE JUST HAD TO TAKE.

THE NEXT STOP WAS THE **GRAND CANYON**. GOING INTO THIS PARK WE WERE FOOLED BY THE "LITTLE COLORADO GORGE". WE TOOK SEVERAL PICTURES BEFORE WE REALIZED WE WERE NOT AT THE CANYON YET.

WE TRIED LIMITING OURSELVES TO NUMBER OF SHOTS PER SITE BUT IT WAS DOWN RIGHT IMPOSSIBLE. WE DIDN'T CARE HOW MANY ROLLS OF FILM WE HAD TO BURY IN OUR BAGS. WHEN YOU GET INTO NATURE AND SHE OPENS HER HEART OUT TO YOU, YOU HAVE TO STAND UP AND TAKE HER PICTURE.

WE STAYED IN THE PARKS CAMP GROUNDS THAT NIGHT AND JACK AND I COULD NOT BELIEVE WHAT WE HAD SEEN. PICTURES CAN'T EXPLAIN THE AWE OF THE CANYON. IF YOU TURN YOUR HEAD, AND THEN LOOK BACK AT THE SAME SPOT YOU WERE JUST LOOKING AT—IT HAS NOW CHANGED. THE COLORS, SHADOWS, WEATHER AND SOUNDS OF THE CANYON CONTINUOUSLY CHANGES THE SCENERY AROUND YOU. IT IS HUMBLING. WE BOTH KNEW IT WAS GOING TO BE TOUGH TO BEAT THIS PLACE, WE WERE WRONG.

DAY 10—AUGUST 19TH, 1971—THURSDAY

ALL THE ELEMENTS AROUND US WAS POINTING TO ANOTHER RAIN FILLED DAY. BUT, AWAY WE WENT. STRAIGHT WEST TO LAS VEGAS, NEVADA. BEFORE WE GOT THERE WE GOT A TREAT THAT WASN'T ON MY LIST. THE "HOOVER DAM". WE JUST LEFT ONE OF NATURES WONDERS AND NOW WE WERE LOOKING AT ONE OF MANS WONDERS.

WE ONLY TOOK A FEW PHOTOS OF THE DAM. LOOKING BACK NOW I WISH WE HAD TAKEN MORE. THE TRAFFIC ACROSS THE DAM WASN'T BAD AT ALL. LOOKING OVER THE SIDES WAS A LITTLE UNSETTLING THOUGH. THE SKY WAS BEGINNING TO GET DARK AND RAIN WAS CLOSE. LAS VEGAS WAS ONLY OVER THE MOUNTAIN AND MY CHAIN WAS STARTING TO WORRY ME. LOTS OF WINDING UP AND DOWN AND IN AND OUT OF THE MOUNTAINS NEEDED TO BE ACCOMPLISHED BEFORE THE RAIN HIT US—SO - AWAY WE WENT. ONE GOOD THING ABOUT THE RAIN WAS IT WAS KEEPING THE TEMPERATURE DOWN TO ABOUT 80 DEGREES. IT MADEFOR A VERY PLEASANT RIDE INTO THE VALLEY OF LAS VEGAS.

THAT'S ALL IT WAS BACK IN 1971—A VALLEY! COMING FROM THE DAM AND HEADING DUE WEST WE CRESTED A HILL CALLED "RAILROAD PASS" AND THERE IT WAS. WAY OFF IN THE DISTANCE THERE WAS A PATCH OF BUILDINGS. PICTURE A ROAD, STRAIGHT AS AN ARROW, DOUBLE LANE, GOING DOWN HILL AND STRAIGHT INTO A CLUMP OF BUILDINGS ABOUT 25 TO 30 MILES DOWN THAT SAME ROAD. FROM THAT VIEW POINT WE COULD SEE THE WHOLE VALLEY. BECAUSE IT WAS DAYLIGHT, THERE WERE NO VISIBLE SIGNS OF LAS VEGAS. TRAVELING DOWN THIS ROAD WE CAME ACROSS A HONDA MOTORCYCLE DEALERSHIP CLOSE TO TOWN. WE DETERMINED IT WAS TIME TO CHANGE THE OILS AND PUT A NEW CHAIN ON MY BIKE. MY RESEARCH ON MOTORCYCLES BEFORE THE TRIP WAS PAYING OFF BIG TIME. I WANTED A BIKE THAT WE COULD GET PARTS FOR— ANYWHERE! SINCE JACK HAD THE SAME BIKE HE PURCHASED A CHAIN ALSO. (SURE ENOUGH—LATER IN THE TRIP AT AROUND THE SAME MILEAGE HE REPLACED HIS TOO) THIS STOP TOOK AROUND ONE AND A HALF HOURS AND IT HAD STARTED RAINING NOW.

THE DARK CLOUDS AND RAIN HAD DIMED THE SUNLIGHT CONSIDERABLY TO A POINT THAT THE LAS VEGAS LIGHTS WERE CATCHING OUR ATTENTION. WE HEADED TOWARDS DOWNTOWN LAS VEGAS. DRIVING THROUGH DOWNTOWN WITH THE COWBOY AND COWGIRL SIGNS WAVING AT US AND HUNDREDS IF NOT THOUSANDS OF LIGHTS FLICKERING OFF AND ON TOOK OUR MINDS OFF THE RAIN. WITH OUR LEATHERS ON AND NOW DRAPPED WITH ADDITIONAL RAINGEAR WE WERE DRAWING ATTENTION

OURSELVES. I REMEMBER GOING TO THE END OF THAT LONG ROAD WE HAD

SEEN HOURS AGO FROM THE TOP OF THE MOUNTAIN, AND JUST DOING A "U"

TURN AND THEN FOLLOWING THE SIGNS TO CALIFORNIA. JACK AND I KNEW

THE SCHEDULE AND NEVER DURING OUR TRIP DID WE ARGUE OR COMPLAIN

ABOUT OUR AGENDA. WE HAD TALKED ABOUT THE IMPORTANCE OF THE

TRIP TO ME, JACK WAS MORE THAN PLEASED JUST TO GO ALONG. THE

POINT IS—WE WERE NOT INTERESTED IN CITIES OR TOWNS OR "LAS

VEGAS"—WE WERE LOOKING FOR THE PICTURESQUE PARTS OF AMERICA.

LITTLE DID WE KNOW THAT LAS VEGAS WOULD BECOME WHAT IT HAS

TODAY.

THE RAIN WAS STARTING TO COME DOWN MORE NOW AND WE WERE IN

THE MIDDLE OF THE DESERT. NO ONE WARNED US OF WHAT WAS ABOUT TO

HAPPEN. YOU SEE - THE SOUTHWEST, ESPECIALLY THE LAS VEGAS AREA,

HAS A LOT OF CLAYS AND CALICHE IN THE SOIL. THIS WE HAD LEARNED AT

ALL THE INDIAN RUINS OVER THE PAST SEVERAL DAYS. WE HAD EVEN

LEARNED HOW THE FAST PACED WATER OF THE COLORADO RIVER HAD

CARVED OUT THE GRAND CANYON. WE DID NOT EXPECT TO EXPERIENCE

THIS AWESOME FORCE FIRST HAND!! IT WAS NOW DUSK AND WE WERE

LOOKING SOUTH AT A TWO LANE HIGHWAY THAT WAS STRAIGHT AS AN

ARROW. THIS ROAD LOOKED SIMULAR TO THE ROAD THAT WE WITNESSED

EARLIER IN THE DAY. THIS TIME HOWEVER, THE ROAD HAD MAJOR—I'M

TALKING SERIOUS DIPS EVERY 100—200 YARDS. NOT ASSOCIATING THIS

WITH ANYTHING I THOUGHT HOW STUPID THE ROAD ENGINEER HAD TO BE

TO LEAVE IT IN THIS CONDITION. AS SOON AS THAT THOUGHT CROSSED MY MIND, MY SIDE VISION CAUGHT SOMETHING STRANGE COME AT US. IT WAS A WALL OF DARK BROWN AND GRAY SOMETHING COMING DOWN AT US THROUGH EACH OF THESE DIPS.

I MUST HAVE SEEN IT FIRST BECAUSE I STOPPED AND JACK WENT ON A LITTLE WAY FURTHER. WE THEN ENDED UP STRANDED BETWEEN THESE DIPS THAT WERE LEFT IN THE CONSTRUCTION OF THESE ROADS. AS HARD AS IT IS TO BELIEVE, THE FLASH FLOOD ENDED AS QUICK AS IT STARTED. WITHIN 15 MINUTES OR SO THE WATER HAD RAN OFF AND WE COULD PROCEED. WHEN WE GOT TO NEEDLES CALIFORNIA IT WAS STILL DRIZZLING.

WE STOPPED AT A FILLING STATION AND ASSESSED THE DAMAGE.

WE WERE BEAT! KICKED! SLAPPED! AND HUNG OUT TO DRY! THAT'S

EXACTLY HOW WE FELT. WE WERE SO TIRED WE FORGOED OUR SIX-PACK

AND PURCHASED TWO BURGERS AND A COKE EACH FOR $.67 EACH. YES,

THAT'S RIGHT, WE ONLY SHELLED OUT ONE DOLLAR AND THIRTY FOUR

CENTS FOR (4) FOUR BURGERS AND (2) TWO COKES. REMEMBER NOW, THIS

WAS 1971. TODAY - THAT'S HOW MUCH ONE COKE IS AT MCDONALDS. THE

BURGER JOINT WAS A BLOCK FROM A REST STATION SO WE HAD A ROOF

OVER OUR HEADS ONCE AGAIN. BY THE TIME WE GOT INTO OUR SLEEPING

BAGS THE RAIN STOPPED. THE AIR WAS DAMP AND COOL; THE NIGHT SKY

OPENED RIGHT UP AND THE STARS WERE EVERYWHERE. WE WENT

THROUGH HELL TODAY, YET WE SAW SO MUCH AND NOW THE DAY WAS

OVER AND IT WAS SO STILL. OUR BODIES WERE HIT HARD TODAY AND THE

SLEEPING BAGS WERE A WELCOMED SITE. WE SLEPT WELL!

CHAPTER 4

DAY 11—AUGUST 20TH, 1971—FRIDAY

WE WOKE UP AFTER WHAT I THOUGHT WAS A GOOD NIGHT OF SLEEP. BEING A MORNING PERSON I WAS LOOKING FORWARD TO THE DAY. JACK ON THE OTHER HAND MUST HAVE SLEPT ON A ROCK OR SOMETHING. WE GOT CROSS WITH EACH OTHER RIGHT OFF THE BAT. WHO KNOWS WHY? MAYBE BECAUSE WE BOTH NEEDED A BATH. FOR WHATEVER REASON WE STAYED APART FROM EACH OTHER. WE GOT ON OUR BIKES AND HEADED SOUTH TO BLYTHE, CALIFORNIA. TOOK A RIGHT TURN AND HEADED WEST TO **JOSHUA TREE NATIONAL MONUMENT**.

NOW, DON'T GET ME WRONG. SOME PEOPLE PROBABLY THINK THIS PLACE IS PICTURESQUE. THE ODD SHAPED TREES THAT CAN BE MISTAKEN FOR CACTUS IS WHAT ALL THE FUSS IS ABOUT. ON THE OTHER HAND COULDN'T FIND ANYTHING TO TAKE A PICTURE OF EXCEPT FOR THE SIGN. SO, WE HEADED FOR L.A. I-10 THROUGH SAN BERNADINO IS A REFRESHING RIDE AFTER BEING IN THE DESERT. BUT THAT WASN'T WHAT WAS KEEPING ME PUMPED UP. ANOTHER ONE OF MY FIRST WAS COMING UP. I—HAD NEVER SEEN THE BEACH. YEA, I WAS IN THE ARMY, AND I WAS STATIONED IN PLACES NEAR THE OCEAN AND YES I HAVE SWAM WITH THE FISHES. I'M TALKING ABOUT THE "CALIFORNIA" BEACHES, YOU KNOW—WHERE THE BEACH BOYS HANG OUT AND ALL THOSE CALIFORNIA GIRLS ARE EVERYWHERE. WE GOT TO THE QUEEN PM.

MARY AROUND 2 P.M. AFTER TAKING A PICTURE OF HER WE FOUND OUR FIRST BEACH! LONG BEACH CALIFORNIA. I COULD COUNT THE GIRLS ON ONE HAND. WE ASK SOMEONE WHATS UP AND THEY SAID IT WAS TOO COLD AND A FRIDAY AFTERNOON. THEY SAID COME BACK IN A FEW HOURS AND THE PLACE WOULD BE PACKED. DO YOU KNOW HOW STUPID THAT

SOUNDED TO TWO GUYS WHO HASN'T STAYED ANYWHERE FOR TWO HOURS.
WE HAD TOO MANY THINGS TO SEE—SO SEE YA! GOOD-BYE BEACH! WE
WERE OFF TO DISNEYLAND.

NO PICTURES ARE NECESSARY; WE HAVE ALL SEEN OR BEEN TO
DISNEYLAND—RIGHT. WELL—NOT THE WAY WE WENT. REMEMBER NOW,
WE NEEDED BATHS, WE HAVEN'T SHAVED SINCE COLORADO, WE'RE STILL
WEARING OUR LEATHERS AND JACK AND I WAS CROSS WITH EACH OTHER
EARLIER IN THE DAY! YEP—IT'S TIME TO PARTY. ENTRANCE TO THE PARK
COST $5.00. WE GOT THERE AT 4 PM AND LEFT AT 12 MIDNIGHT. MOM'S
WERE GRABING THEIR KIDS, PARENTS WERE WATCHING THEIR DAUGHTERS
AND WE HAD SECURITY PEOPLE AROUND US ALL NIGHT. IT DID NOT STOP
US ONE BIT. ONCE INSIDE THE PARK WE WERE KIDS AGAIN. WE ROAD AS
MANY RIDES AS POSSIBLE AND EVEN MET A FEW GIRLS. BUT—THAT'S
ANOTHER STORY…

DAY 12—AUGUST 21ST, 1971—SATURDAY

JACK BLAMED IT ON THE SIX-PACK, I BLAMED IT ON LAST NIGHTS
COMPANY—BUT WE GOT A LATE START ANYWAY. (WHICH HAPPENS TO BE
THE END OF THE PREVIOUS "THAT'S ANOTHER STORY) WE DIDN'T GET UP
UNTIL 10 AM. BUT EVEN AT 10 AM IT WAS A NICE 75—80 DEGREE OUT AND
THE SKY WAS FINALLY CLEAR. ALL IN ALL IT MADE FOR SOME GOOD
TIMING. WE WANTED TO HIT **<u>DEATH VALLEY</u>** AT THE PEAK OF THE
AFTERNOON TO REALLY EXPERIENCE THE ELEMENTS. BAD MISTAKE!!!! THE

TEMPERATURE WAS 120 +! THERE WAS NOTHING WRONG WITH MY CAMERA. AND, IN OUR LEATHERS YOU CAN IMAGINE THE OVEN WE WERE IN. WE WERE LOSING A LOT OF FLUIDS AND IT FELT LIKE IT WAS ALL IN THE BOTTOM OF MY BOOTS. WE DIDN'T DARE TAKE OFF ANYTHING BECAUSE THE SUN WOULD COOK US MORE. HALF WAY THROUGH WE STOPPED AT THE PARK STATION AND BOUGHT A COKE AND ICE CREAM BAR. DRANK LOTS OF WATER AND BOTH JACK AND I TOOK A TOWEL AND SOAKED IT IN WATER AND COVERED OUR HEADS WITH IT. WHEN I PUT MY HELMET ON THE EXCESS WATER IN THE TOWEL SQUEEZED OUT AND RAN DOWN MY BACK—IT FELT GOOD. I QUESS WE COULD HAVE STAYED AND LOOKED AT "NOTHING" BUT WE KNEW THE MOUNTAINS WERE ONLY A FEW HOURS AWAY. ON THE WAY OUT OUR TOWELS TURNED TO CARDBOARD, OR SO IT SEEMED, AND IT FELT LIKE IT WAS GETTING HOTTER. WE NOW KNEW WHY THE RANGER WAS A LITTLE CONCERNED ABOUT US GOING ON. MY GLOVES, BLACK LEATHER, WERE LIKE A HOT IRON. MY TOES INSIDE MY BLACK ARMY BOOTS WERE TRYING VERY MUCH NOT TO TOUCH THE INSIDE OF THE BOOT, THE HEAT WAS GOING RIGHT THROUGH THE LEATHER. YOU CAN IMAGINE THE COMFORT IN SEEING THE SIERRA NEVADA MOUNTAIN RANGE INCHING TOWARDS US.

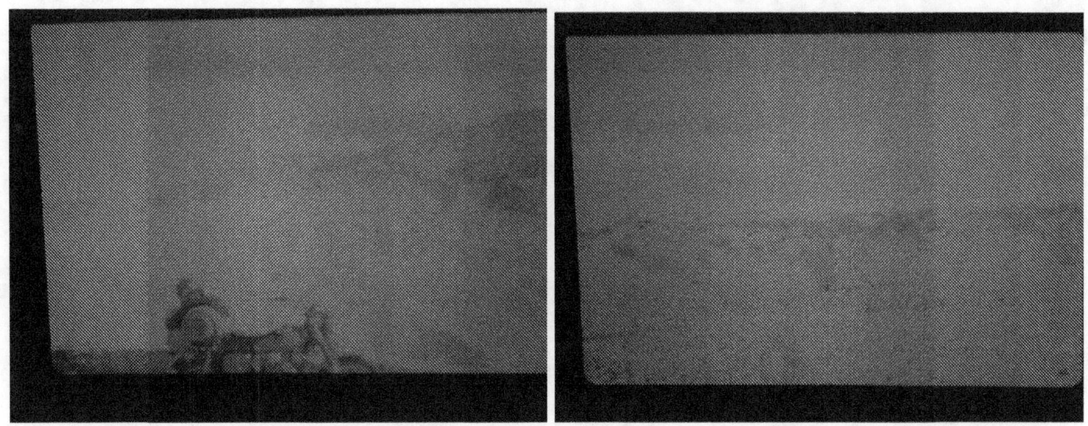

WE GASED UP IN INDEPENDENCE, CALIFORNIA AFTER RIDING FOR THE PAST HALF HOUR AT THE FOOT OF THE SIERRA NEVADA'S; WHICH WAS VERY CALMING COMPARED TO ONLY AN HOUR OR SO AGO WE WERE AT A MINUS 200 FOOT ELEVATION. JACK SAID HE THOUGHT HE WENT THROUGH ARMY TRAINING TO PREPARE HIM FOR COMBAT—IT TURNSOUT HE NEEDED THE TRAINING FOR OUR TRIP. WHILE FILLING OUR TANKS UP WE GOT A CLOSE LOOK AT WHAT THE HEAT HAD DONE TO OUR BODIES. JACK'S FACE WAS BEET RED AND LOOKING IN THE MIRROR I WAS GLAD WE HAD BEEN GROWING OUR BEARDS. MY FOREHEAD, HOWEVER, WAS UNPROTECTED. WE JOTTED SOME NOTES IN OUR JOURNALS AND BOTH LOOKED UP AT EACH OTHER AT THE SAME TIME WHEN WE NOTICED OUR NEXT STOP. "**<u>DEVILS POST PILE</u>**"! NOW WE'RE GUYS, AND WE ARE SUPPOSE TO BE TOUGH, OR AT LEAST ACT TOUGH, BUT, NOT KNOWING WHAT THE HELL "DEVILS POST PILE" MEANT, IT WAS DECIDED TO WAIT UNTIL TOMORROW TO PUT OURSELVES THROUGH ANYMORE TORTURE. SO - - - BEER TIME! WE GRABBED A HAMBURGER NEAR THE FILLING STATION AND WATCHED THE SUN GO DOWN OVER THE MOUNTAINS.

CHAPTER 5

DAY 13—AUGUST 22ND, 1971—SUNDAY

SOME MORNINGS IT WAS JUST LIKE HEAVEN! WE WOULD WAKE UP IN AN

UNBELIEVABLE PLACE AFTER STOPPING WELL AFTER THE SUN WENT DOWN

THE PREVIOUS NIGHT. THIS MORNING WAS ONE OF THEM. THE DRASTIC

CHANGE IN COLORS FROM DEATH VALLEY TO THE MOUNTAINS AND

COMING FROM THE VERY DRY HEAT TO NOW THE MOIST COOL AIR. WE

EVEN SAW LOTS OF LIFE AROUND US. WITH OUR FOREHEADS ALREADY

CRACKING FROM THE SUN BURN OF YESTERDAY NOTHING WAS EVER

39

MENTIONED BETWEEN US ABOUT THE PAST. IT WAS EVIDENT AS SOON AS

WE OPENED OUR EYES THIS MORNING THAT THERE WAS A LOT MORE TO SEE

AHEAD OF US. THIS MOUNTAIN RANGE HAS A BEAUTY WHICH IS HARD TO

DISCRIBE. CRISP, COMES TO MIND.

    IT TURNS OUT THAT WE HAD VERY LITTLE IF ANYTHING TO BE ALARMED

ABOUT OUR NEXT STOP—"**<u>DEVILS POST PILE</u>**". IT WAS ASTONISHING IN IT'S

OWN RIGHT BUT NOT ALARMING BY ANY STANDARDS. IT WAS HOWEVER A

PRELUDE TO WHAT WAS TO BE. OUR NEXT STOP WAS "**<u>YOSEMITE</u>**".

LOOKING BACK NOW IT WAS MY #1 PICK. JACK'S #1 PICK COMES LATER.

THE LONG ROAD UP THE SIDE OF THE MOUNTAIN ON A 350 HONDA SENT

IMAGES BACK TO PREVIOUS MOUNTAIN AREAS WE HAD BEEN IN. YOU NEED

TO MAGNIFY THOSE SPOTS BY 2 OR MAYBE 3 TO COME CLOSE TO

"YOSEMITE". THE COLORS OF THE PARK AND FRESHNESS IS UNMATCHED.

THE SMOOTH, AT TIMES, BALD TOP MOUNTAINS SHOW BOLD AND MAJESTIC

FORTITUDE WHILE THE STREAMS AND MOSS COVERED ROCKS SHOW

PERSISTANCE AND DETERMINATION; I QUICKLY REACHED OVER MY BACK

AND TOUCHED THE FLAG THAT I PROUDLY WORE. CAMERAS OR SOME SORT

OF COPY MATERIAL IS NEEDED TO TRY TO CAPTURE THE RICH COLORS—I

DON'T THINK THERE IS COLORS LIKE THESE ON AN ARTIST PALETTE.

THE WATER FALLS, CANYONS AND JUST THE WHOLE PARK TAKES ON A

NEW MEANING WHEN YOU FIND OUT IT ONLY OPENS A FEW MONTHS OF THE

YEAR.

DOWN THE MOUNTAIN WE WENT WITH THE CALIFORNIA WINE VALLEY

IN FRONT OF US. NEITHER JACK OR I LIKE WINE, SO NO PROLONGED VISITS

ENSUED, BUT WE, OR I, GOT AN UNEXPECTED VISIT. I REMEMBER RIDING

THROUGH ROWS OF GRAPE VINES WHEN SUDDENLY I FELT A SHARP NEEDLE

LIKE OBJECT PENITRATE MY UPPER ARM. MY REFLECTS SLAPPED AT IT AND

THAT JUST SEEMED TO MAKE THE OBJECT PICK ANOTHER SPOT. AFTER TWO

OR THREE ATTEMPTS TO STOP WHATEVER WAS NOW CAUSEING GREAT PAIN, I THEN GRABBED AND SQUEEZED REAL HARD. YOU SEE—MY LEATHERS WERE OPEN SLEEVED AND MY ARMS WERE EXTENDED COMFORTABLY TO THE HANDLEBARS. THIS MUST HAVE MADE AN ATTRACTIVE LOOKING DWELLING FOR A BUMBLE BEE. YES—A BIG YELLOW AND BLACK, FAT, BUMBLE BEE. NOW, I'M SURE THESE GUYS ARE NATURES HELPERS AND VERY NICE ANIMALS BUT WHEN THE FIGHT BROKE OUT HE DIDN'T KNOW WHAT WAS HAPPENING TO HIM AND I LIKEWISE WAS DEFENDING MYSELF. ENOUGH SAID!—OF COURSE JACK WAS LAUGHING THE WHOLE TIME! NO MORE THAN 10—20 MINUTES LATER MY CHAIN BROKE. NO PROBLEM! CHANGING OR TAKING OUT A LINK IN OUR CHAINS BECAME A SMALL SET BACK OF 30 OR SO MINUTES THROUGHOUT THE TRIP. JACK TOOK THIS TIME TO PUT HIS NEW CHAIN ON; THE ONE HE BOUGHT IN LAS VEGAS. NONE OF THESE SMALL PROBLEMS FAZED US, WE NEW A SHOWER WAS IN STORE FOR US THIS EVENING.

ONE OF THE THINGS WE DID BEFORE STARTING OUR TRIP WAS TO ADD FRIENDS AND RELATIVES AROUND THE TRIP ROUTE. TONIGHT WE WOULD BE IN SAN JOSE, CALIFORNIA. AN ARMY BUDDY OF OURS HAD A SHOWER, DINNER, PARTY AND SISTER WAITING FOR US - BUT, THAT'S ANOTHER STORY.

DAY 14—AUGUST 23RD, 1971—MONDAY

AFTER BREAKFAST WITH THE GIRLS WE HAD TO STOP AT HONDA SHOP

BECAUSE DURING THE FIGHT WITH THE BUMBLE BEE I BROKE MY BREAK

LEVER.

THE GOLDEN GATE BRIDGE AND ALCATRAZ ISLAND ARE FAMILIAR

SHOTS FOR ANY TOURIST. IT WAS ONLY PROPER WE FOLLOWED THE CROWD

ON THIS MORNING. THE SAN FRANCISCO SKYLINE HOWEVER WASN'T ON

OUR NATIONAL PARKS LIST SO AWAY WE WENT.

JUST ON THE OTHER SIDE OF THE GOLDEN GATE IS **MUIR WOODS**. THIS IS

A SMALL PARK IN COMPARISON TO SOME THAT WE HAD BEEN THOUGH.

NEVERTHELESS, WELL WORTH OUR PARKING OF OUR BIKES AND STROLLING THROUGH WITH ALL THE OTHER TOURIST.

JUST AFTER STOPPING FOR GAS AT GRIDLEY, CALIFORNIA WE CAME ACROSS MORE ORCHARDS OF VARIOUS FRUITS. I REMEMBER SEVERAL DROPPING INTO OUR BAGS AS WE PASSED UNDER THEM—BUT THAT'S ANOTHER STORY.

THE SUN WAS SETTING AND WE HAD LOTS OF MILES BEFORE OUR NEXT STOP. "**LASSEN VOLCANIC NATIONAL PARK**". WITH THAT IN MIND MY BREAKS WERE ON AGAIN. WE HAD BEEN FOLLOWING A RIVER FOR THE PAST 10 MILES OR SO AND IT KEPT CALLING OUR NAMES.

WE USUALLY ROAD INTO THE NIGHT TO GET CLOSE TO OUR NEXT STOP.

THIS SPOT JUST WAS TOO MUCH TO PASS UP. WE HAD A GOOD HOUR OR SO

OF SUNLIGHT AND IT MADE FOR A PERFECT OPPORTUNITY TO CLEAN UP

AND PICK A FAVORABLE CAMP SITE. WE EVEN HAD ENOUGH TIME TO WRITE

SOME POSTCARDS AND CATCH UP ON OUR JOURNALS. WE SCOUTED

AROUND AND FOUND SOME BERRIES AND STARTED A NICE CAMPFIRE. NO

RAIN, OPEN SKIES, THE SOUND OF A RIVER BESIDE US—IT WAS TIME FOR A

PEACEFUL NIGHT. WELL—

DAY 15—AUGUST 24TH, 1971—TUESDAY

WE SHOULD HAVE HAD A SIX-PACK LAST NIGHT! MAYBE, JUST MAYBE

WE WOULD HAVE SLEPT THROUGH IT. AT AROUND 5 A.M A LOUD SQUEEL

WITH A SNORTING AT THE END WOKE BOTH OF US UP SIMOTANEOUSLY.

BEING THE BIG, TOUGH MEN WE WERE, JACK SPOKE FIRST TO SAY THAT HE

HAD A VERY RESTFUL EVENING AND HE FELT WE SHOULD GET AN EARLY

START. I WAS NOT ABOUT TO ARGUE, AND TO THIS DAY, NEITHER OF US

TELL THE STORY THE SAME WAY.

ANYWAY—WE GOT ON OUR BIKES AND ROAD A GOOD 30 MILES OR SO

BEFORE WE NOTICED THE EARLY MORNINGS WERE GETTING CHILLY. WE

HAD TO TAKE A QUICK STOP TO ADD A FEW MORE LAYERS OF CLOTHS AND

DIG OUT OUR GLOVES AND JACK ADDED A FACE SHIELD TO HIS HELMET.

<u>LASSEN VOLCANIC NATIONAL PARK</u> WAS NOTHING LIKE WHAT WE EXPECTED. HOT SPRINGS AND BEAUTIFUL MOUNTAIN VISTAS ARE CONTRARY TO THE TITLE. THE VISITOR CENTER SET US STRAIGHT. ON THE MAP YOU CAN TELL WE TOOK QUITE A DETOUR TO GET THERE AND THE VOTE WAS UNANIMOUS—IT WAS WORTH THE EXTRA MILES. COMING BACK DOWN THE MOUNTAIN WE CAME UP ON A SCENIC OUTLOOK. YOU'VE SEEN THEM—NICELY CARVED OUT AND STRATEGICALLY PLACED SO THE PUBLIC CAN GET THERE BEST PICTURE. NORMALLY WE WOULD HAVE STOPPED. IN FACT WE PULLED INTO, BUT ONLY SLOWED DOWN. THERE WERE ABOUT 8 OR 10 "HELL'S ANGELS" TAKING A BREAK FROM THERE RIDE AND A FEW WERE HAVING NO PROBLEM MOTIONING US OVER AND CALLING US SWEET THINGS LIKE—"LOOK AT THE MOMAS"—"COOL DUDES ON THE MINI-BIKES". THIS WAS ANOTHER ONE OF THOSE MOMENTS WHEN NEITHER ONE OF US

WANTED TO PROVE OUR MANHOOD. SO—WE CONTINUED DOWN THE HILL.

WHEN WE GOT TO REDDING, CALIFORNIA WE HAD TO STOP FOR GAS. GUESS

WHO WAS BEHIND US. IT DIDN'T LOOK GOOD! SINCE WE WERE OFF OUR

BIKES AND ALREADY IN THE MOTIONS OF FILLING UP—WE HOPED FOR THE

BEST. IT STARTED - - - "WHERE U MOMAS GOING? TO A BAKE SALE"? "HOW

MANY SQUIRLS DOES IT TAKE TO KEEP ONE OF THOSE THINGS RUNNING"?

BUT THEN—ONE OF THE GUYS SAW OUR LICENSE PLATES AND THEY DID A

180. IT WENT FROM BANTING US TO REALLY DEEP INTEREST. "WOW, MAN—

YOU'RE A LONG WAY FROM HOME, DUDE". NOT WANTING THE MOOD TO

CHANGE AGAIN WE PICKED OUR SPOT IN THE CONVERSATION TO GET THE

HELL OUT OF THERE.

THE NEXT STOP WAS ON THE CALIFORNIA COASTLINE. COMING OFF OF

299 WE MADE A RIGHT TURN AT ARCATA, CALIFORNIA. OKAY, WE SAW THE

OCEAN IN L.A. AND WE EVEN GOT OFF OUR BIKES TO WALK ON THE BEACH,

BUT, TO RIDE ON 101 ON A COOL DAY IS BREATHTAKING. THE WEATHER

WAS PERFECT AND WE STILL HAD OUR MANHOOD EVEN THOUGH IT HAD

BEEN TESTED TWICE IN ONE DAY. WOW, WHAT A DAY! AND NOW, WE WERE

ABOUT TO BE HUMBLED ONCE AGAIN.

THE **<u>REDWOOD FOREST</u>** WAS AWESOME. WE DIDN'T GO INTO THE PARK BECAUSE OF THE $1.25 PER PERSON FEE. BESIDES, WE WERE ABLE TO RIDE THROUGH LOT'S OF THE TREES ON HIGHWAY 101. THE TREES WE SAW WERE LARGE ENOUGH TO DRIVE THROUGH, AND WE DID GO THROUGH ONE.

WELL—IT WAS TIME TO SAY GOODBYE FOR NOW TO THE OCEAN. WE HAD

TO MAKE A RIGHT TURN AT CRESENT CITY ON 199 EAST TO MAKE OUR WAY

TO TOMORROWS DESTINATION OF "**CRATER LAKE**". WE WERE GETTING

TIRED AND A SIX-PACK WAS DEFINITELY ON OUR MINDS, SO, SOMEWHERE

NEAR I-5 WE WERE CLOSE TO ANOTHER STREAM. WE HAD ALREADY

STOPPED AND FUELED UP FOR THE EVENING AND GOT THE BEER SO WE

TOOK THE FIRST PATH TOWARDS THE STREAM THE PATH TOOK US OVER A

FEW LOW POINTS WITH WATER AND I LOST IT! NOW, DON'T TELL ANYONE,

BUT WHEN A GUY WHO HAS BEEN RIDEING BIKES ALL HIS LIFE DUMPS HIS—

IT'S JUST NOT RIGHT!!! NO MORE THAN 20 FEET LATER JACK DROPS HIS.

SO—WE DID WHAT ANY RED BLOODED BOY WOULD—WE BLAMED IT ON

THE MUD! TO BED WE WENT.

DAY 16—AUGUST 25TH, 1971—WEDNESDAY

THE SITE WE HAPPENED UPON REWARDED US WITH BLACK BERRIES

EVERYWHERE. AFTER SEVERAL HAND FULLS WE HEADED OUT. THE FIRST

GAS STATION WE STOPPED AT WAS IN PROSPECT, OREGON. WE PURCHASED

SOME MILK AND INSTANT BREAKFAST MIX AT A STORE AND THAT MIXED

WELL WITH THE BERRIES WE HAD EARLIER. THE DAY WAS ALREADY

TURNING OUT BETTER THAN THE DAY BEFORE. IT WAS A GOOD THING THAT

NEITHER JACK OR I RESEARCHED THE PLACES WE HAD MARKED ON THE

MAP. I JUST FOUND A MAP AND CIRCLED ANY N.P. OR S.P. SYMBOL AND

THEN DREW A LINE THAT WOULD CATCH THE MOST OF THEM. THE POINT

I'M TRYING TO MAKE IS THAT WE WERE SURPRISED IN MOST CASES

BECAUSE WE HAD ONE EXPECTATION AND IT USUALLY TURNED OUT AS

SOMETHING ENTIRELY DIFFERENT.

   "**<u>CRATER LAKE NATIONAL PARK</u>**" IS AN EXAMPLE OF THIS

MISUNDERSTANDING. I SAW IN MY MIND A BIG HOLE WITH WATER IN IT. IT

TURNED OUT TO BE AND EXTINCT VOLCANO WITH A LAKE INSIDE WITH

ANOTHER VOLCANO CONE STARTING AGAIN! THE SCENERY WAS ONCE

AGAIN BREATHTAKING. JACK AND I FOUND OURSELVES WONDERING WHEN

WE WOULD STOP BEING IMPRESSED. THE ALTITUDE, AND DISTANCE FROM

ANY MAJOR CITY, CERTAINLY HELPED—BUT STILL, THE AIR AND

BRILLIANCE OF COLORS WERE APPRECIATED.

   THE HIGH ELEVATION WAS ALSO CHANGING OUR ENGINES FEELINGS.

MY BIKE WAS STARTING TO MISS AND JACK DIDN'T FEEL COMFORTABLE

WITH THE POWER OF HIS EITHER. SO—AT OUR NEXT GAS STATION IN

OAKRIDGE, OREGON WE CHANGED OUR PLUGS AND OIL. THAT DID THE

TRICK. WE THEN HAD A STRAIGHT RIDE NORTH, PAST EUGENE, THEN SALEM

AND INTO OREGON CITY. FREEWAY RIDING DIDN'T USUALLY APPEAL TO US,

BUT TODAY IT WAS JUST MEANT TO BE. BECAUSE OUR BIKES WERE RUNNING SO GOOD.

WE STOPPED AND GOT GAS AND THIS TIME SOME LUNCH MEAT AND BREAD. WE MADE SANDWICHES OUT OF THE WHOLE LOAF AND RETURNED EACH ONE BACK INSIDE THE SAME BAG AND SAVED FOR LATER. WE LEFT OREGON CITY AND MADE A LEFT AT PORTLAND AND HEADED TOWARDS THE COASTLINE. THE SUN WAS SETTING SO WE KNEW THERE WAS NO CHANCE OF MAKING IT TONIGHT. IT BECAME PITCH BLACK OUTSIDE WITH THE FOG ROLLING IN. WE HAD TO SLOW DOWN TO AROUND 15—20 MPH BECAUSE OUR HEADLIGHTS WERE BOUNCHING BACK AT US AND WE WEREN'T MAKING ANY PROGRESS. WE FOUND A SPOT AND DRUG OUR BAGS OUT, WRAPPED UP AND WENT TO SLEEP.

DAY 17—AUGUST 26TH, 1971—THURSDAY

THINK BACK ON THOSE SATURDAY OR SUNDAY MORNINGS WHEN YOU KNOW YOU NEED TO GET UP BUT YOU JUST LAY THERE ANOTHER 15 MINUTES. YOUR SO COMFORTABLE AND YOU'VE GOT THE COVERS ALL AROUND YOU JUST TO THE PERFECT TEMPERATURE—WHEN - - - RINGGG, OR IN OUR CASE HONKKKKKKKKKKKKKKK - WE HAD WOKE UP TO A SEMI TRUCKS HORN THAT WAS TRYING TO SCAR A DEER FROM THE ROAD.

I WAS UP AND LOOKING FOR MY RIFLE AND WONDERING WHICH WAY THE THE ENEMY WAS COMING FROM AND THEN I NOTICED JACK HADN'T EVEN MOVED. I GOT MY CAMERA AND WAITED FOR HIS HEAD TO COME UP. THE PICTURE SAYS IT ALL. WE HAD PARKED ON A FREEWAY MOUNTAIN-CUT OUT AND WAS ONLY 10—20 FEET FROM THE EDGE. THE FOG WAS SO THICK THE NIGHT BEFORE AND NO TRAFFIC AT ALL SO WE HAD NO IDEA. IT DIDN'T TAKE MUCH IMAGINATION TO KNOW WHAT WOULD HAVE HAPPENED IF EITHER OF US WOULD HAVE HAD A RESTLESS NIGHT AND ROLLED A LITTLE!!!?

WE GOT ON OUR WAY AND OUR FIRST STOP WAS FT. **CLATSOP NATIONAL MONUMENT**. MY HISTORY TEACHERS WOULD BE SURPRISED

THAT I WAS INTERESTED IN ANY KIND OF HISTORY. BUT THIS CLASS WAS

DIFFERENT.

LEWIS AND CLARK ENDED UP HERE ON THERE EXPEDITION AND JACK

AND I HAD MADE IT ALSO. THE FORT WAS WELL MAINTAINED AND THE

DEER AND OTHER WILDLIFE WERE RUNNING AROUND EVERYWHERE.

WE THEN TOOK OFF TO MAKE A LOOP AROUND THE OLYMPIC

PENINSULA. TODAYS RIDE WAS FABULOUS. WE STAYED ON 101 AND THE

OCEAN WAS IN OUR SIGHT FOR MOST OF THE DAY. A FEW STOPS ALONG THE

SHORE LINE AND RUNNING IN AND OUT OF THE **OLYMPIC NATIONAL PARK**

SLOWED OUR SPEED WAY DOWN. IT WAS ONE OF THOSE DAYS THAT MILES

GAVE WAY TO BEAUTY.

CHAPTER 6

DAY 18—AUGUST 27TH, 1971—FRIDAY

TODAY WE START OUR JOURNEY IN A NEW DIRECTION—EAST! WE WOKE UP STILL IN OLYMPIC NATIONAL PARK AND THE SCENERY WAS JUST AS BEAUTIFUL AS THE DAY BEFORE. YET—WE KNEW THE COAST WOULD BE OUT OF SITE AND NEW EXPERIENCES WERE RIGHT AROUND THE CORNER.

IT DIDN'T TAKE LONG—JACK OPENED HIS SLEEPING BAG AND SMELLED THE FIRST BREATH OF COOL, MOIST AIR THAT WAS NOT RAIN BUT PUDDLES OF DEW ALL AROUND AND ON US. OH YES, I FORGOT, THE PUDDLES ALSO HAD SLIMY GREEN THINGS IN THEM. WITH A LITTLE MORE INSPECTION WE FOUND THEM EVERYWHERE. IN OUR HELMETS, OUR BOOTS, OUR LEATHERS AND ALL OVER OUR BIKES. THEY LOOKED LIKE A DOUBLE PIECE OF CHEWED BUBBLE GUM (EXCEPT GREEN) THAT MOVES. IF YOU TAKE THE SHELL OFF A SNAIL AND FATTEN HIM UP A BIT, HE COULD BE ONE OF THESE GUYS RELATIVES. YUCK!!!

TO TOP IT OFF, OUR BIKES WERE COLD AND NOT RUNNING RIGHT. MINE FINALLY STARTED AND WE PUSH STARTED JACKS. HWY.101 TOOK US TO OLYMPIA, WASHINGTON AND WE DETOURED A LITTLE TO SEE THE STATE CAPITAL BUILDING. A GAS STATION ATTENDENT SAID WE SHOULD NOT MISS IT BECAUSE IT WAS MADE OF MARBLE.

WE DIDN'T NEED A MAP OR ATTENDENT TO TELL WHERE OUR NEXT STOP WAS. IT STOOD PROUD AND BOLD FOR ALL TO SEE.

<u>MOUNT RAINIER NATIONAL PARK</u> LIKE MANY OF THE OTHERS REQUIRES MORE THAN A DAY TO DISCOVER HER. THE VAST VALLEYS AND ENDLESS PICTURE POINTS DEFY ANYONE TO ONLY MAKE A QUICK RUN THROUGH. BUT, THAT IS JUST WHAT WE DID! THE WEATHER HAD TURNED NASTY. IT WASN'T RAINING, BUT THE AIR WAS THICK AND SO CLAMY WE FELT WE WERE IN A SHOWER. IT WAS UNFORTUNATE THAT WE WERE GIVING WAY TO OUR UNCOMFORTABLE SETTING BECAUSE EVERYWHERE YOU LOOKED WAS A POSTCARD. WE HAD TO FIGHT THE SLICK ROADS ALL THE WAY DOWN AND ALL THE TIME WIPING THE WATER OFF OUR SHIELDS. IF WE WEREN'T SO COLD WE PROBABLY WOULD HAVE STOPPED AND CAMPED OUT. SOMEWHERE PAST YAKIMA WE FOUND ANOTHER RIVER AND SETTLED IN FOR THE NIGHT.

DAY 19—AUGUST 28TH, 1971—SATURDAY

WE STARTED FOR SPOKANE, WASHINGTON EARLY AS USUAL AND

CROSSED THE COLUMBIA RIVER.

I WAS DEEP IN THOUGHT WHEN JACK TOOK MY CAMERA AND CAUGHT

ME OFF GUARD. I LATER TOLD HIM I WAS THINKING OF HOW I WAS GOING

TO HANDLE THE REST OF MY LIFE. I'VE ALWAYS SAID LIFE IS A GAME.

SOME WIN, SOME LOSE. I KNEW IF I COULD LEARN THE RULES I WOULD

BECOME A BETTER PLAYER. BUT—THAT'S ANOTHER STORY.

THE SUN WAS OUT AND WE WERE DRY. RICHARD WAS FEELING HIS OATS.

ON THE ROAD WITH NOTHING TO DO I WAS GOOFING OFF WHEN MY HANDLE

BAR CAME WITHIN INCHES OF JACKS. MAYBE LESS THAN AN INCH AT 55—60 MPH ON I—90. JACK WASN'T AMUSSED—ENOUGH SAID. I WAS GETTING ALL CHARGED UP BECAUSE MY UNCLE LIVED IN KELLOGG, IDAHO WHICH WAS JUST DOWN THE ROAD. A HOT SHOWER, HOT FOOD AND A NICE EVENING WITH RELATIVES. ON THE WAY WE STOPPED AT CLIFF PARK IN SPOKANE AND ATE SOME APPLES THAT FELL OFF SOME TREES IN THE PARK. (SURE)

JACK STARTED TO TAKE A PICTURE AND HIS CAMERA WOULDN'T WORK. WE WERE LUCKY IT WAS SATURDAY AND BEFORE NOON BECAUSE THE SHOP WE FOUND CLOSED AT NOON. WE TOOK THE TIME TO GRAB A BEER AND JUST CHILL OUT FOR A HOUR OR SO.

WHEN WE GOT TO KELLOGG MY UNCLE WAS NOT IN SO WE BOUGHT SOME GROCERIES AND WENT TO THE NEAREST CAMP SITE. THE $1.00 PER PERSON WAS VERY ATTRACTIVE SINCE WE NEEDED A SHOWER.

DAY 20—AUGUST 29TH, 1971—SUNDAY

WE WERE CLEANED UP AND READY TO RIDE. THE DAY FELT GOOD BUT BY 10 A.M. IT WAS RAINING ON US AGAIN. WHEN WE GOT TO **<u>BIG HOLE BATTLEFIELD NATIONAL MONUMENT</u>** PICTURES WOULD NOT WORK. IT HAD TURNED DARK AND THE RAIN WAS STEADY. WE DID ENJOY THE PRESENTATION AT THE VISITORS CENTER, IT WAS MOST INFORMATIVE AND WE ACTUALLY TOOK TIME TO LISTEN.

WE HEADED SOUTH ON 93 BACK INTO IDAHO AND STOPPED IN GIBBONSVILLE THEN CHALLIS AND THEN ARCO, IDAHO FOR GAS. WE

FINALLY OUT RAN THE RAIN RIGHT BEFORE ARCO. THAT WAS PERFECT

TIMING BECAUSE OUR NEXT STOP WAS ONLY A FEW MILES AWAY.

<u>CRATERS OF THE MOON NATIONAL MONUMENT</u> IS A VERY EERY

PLACE. PICTURE A FLAT DESERT EXCEPT EVERYTHING IS DARK, DARK

BROWN. LAVA FLOWS THAT CREATED THIS AREA HAS ALLOWED VERY

LITTLE TO COME BACK. EVIDENCE OF THESE FLOWS ARE EVERYWHERE.

THE MOST NOTIBLE ARE THE TREES THAT HAVE BEEN TWISTED AND

TURNED INTO PETRIFIED WOOD.

WE WERE SPOILED BY THE PARK WE STAYED IN LAST NIGHT SO WE TRIED

ANOTHER ONE. THE COST OF THIS ONE WAS DOUBLE - $2.00 PER PERSON

WITH NO FACILITIES, WE ROAD ON. WE CAMPED OUT AND MY LOG SHOWS I

ATE A CAN OF BEANS, 3 COOKIES, TURKEY SLICES AND CHOCOLATE MILK.

HEY, WHAT HAPPENED TO THE BEER?

DAY 21—AUGUST 30TH, 1971—MONDAY

   JACK WAS UP FIRST AND MAKING ALL KINDS OF RACKET. HE SAYS HE

WAS SINGING BUT WE ALL KNOW HE CHOSE ANOTHER FIELD TO MAKE A

LIVING. HE WAS LIKE A YOUNG COLT, SKIPPING AROUND AND JABBING AT

ME—IT MUST HAVE BEEN THE CHOCOLATE MILK. (HE'S FROM WISCONSIN)

   WE DROVE INTO IDAHO FALLS AND TO MY SURPRISE JACK BOUGHT

BREAKFEAST—YES FEAST! HE CAME CLEAN, HE HAD BEEN WAITING THE

WHOLE TRIP TO SEE YELLOWSTONE. HE COULDN'T QUIT TALKING. HE

HURRIED ME BACK ONTO OUR BIKES AND AWAY WE WENT.

5 AND ½ MILES DOWN THE ROAD I RAN OUT OF GAS!!!! BY MY RECORDS I SHOULD HAVE BEEN ABLE TO GO ANOTHER 30—45 MILES. BUT, I HAD A LEAK AND IT WAS MONDAY AND ALL HONDA SHOPS ARE CLOSED ON MONDAYS. JACK DROVE BACK TO IDAHO FALLS FOR GAS AND AFTER FILLING MY TANK WE THEN HAD TO RETURN THE GAS CAN!

STARTED BACK ON THE ROAD AND I ALMOST HAD A WREAK WHEN ANOTHER BUBBLE BEE WENT DOWN MY SHIRT. JACK WAS STARTING TO WONDER IF I WAS TRYING TO SPOIL HIS DAY. JACKS DAY WAS SAVED WHEN WE GOT OUR FIRST SIGHT OF THE **GRAND TETONS**. FOR THOSE OF YOU WHO HAVE STOOD BELOW THEM THEY ARE INSPIRING! MANY, MANY ARTIST HAVE CAPTURED THEM ON CANVAS.

THE REASON IS THAT THESE MOUNTAINS PULL YOU IN. THEY REACH OUT AND "DARE" YOU TO ENTER! THAT'S A POWERFUL WORD TO A LOT OF PEOPLE. THIS MOUNTAIN RANGE IS ONLY A WARM UP TO WHAT WE WERE ABOUT TO SEE. JACK HAD EVERY REASON TO CALL **YELLOWSTONE NATIONAL PARK** HIS FAVORITE. ENTERING THE PARK THE FIRST THING WE SAW WAS A SHOWER ROOM AND LAUNDRY ROOM. WE TOOK A GOOD HOUR

AND A HALF TO CLEAN UP AND GET ON THE WAY. THE WATER FALLS AND

GEYSERS AND NATURAL WONDERS ABOUND IN THIS PARK.

WE WERE USE TO DRIVING MILES BETWEEN SITES BUT IN YELLOWSTONE

IT'S LIKE BEING IN A SHOPPING MALL. EACH TIME YOU PASS A STORE

ANOTHER ONE COMPLETELY DIFFERENT IN NATURE IS RIGHT THERE. WE

WERE SCARED WE WOULD USE UP ALL OF OUR FILM.

NOT ONLY DID WE SEE NATURE, NATURE STARTED LOOKING BACK AT US. THIS WAS THE FEATHER THAT WAS TICKLING JACK ALL MORNING. HE HAD HEARD ALL HIS LIFE IF HE WANTED TO SEE A BEAR HE NEEDED TO GO TO YELLOWSTONE. WE TURNED THE CORNER AND NOTICED A LINE OF CARS WAS PARKED ALONG THE ROADWAY. WE TURNED OUR BIKES OFF AND GOT OUR CAMERAS OUT. MOTHERS KEPT THERE KIDS CLOSE WHILE ALL THE AMATURE CAMERAMAN WERE MAKING KODACK RICH.

THIS BEAR HAD BEEN PHOTOGRAPHED SO MANY TIMES I BET HE WOULD HAVE GIVEN US HIS AUTOGRAPH. WE SHOULD HAVE LEARNED OUR LEASON WITH THE BEAR BECAUSE JUST DOWN THE ROAD WE CAME ACROSS SOME ELK. JACK AND I, BEING FIRST THERE, SPENT ABOUT 30 MINUTES OR SO ON

OUR HANDS AND KNEES GETTING CLOSE ENOUGH TO TAKE SOME NEAT

PICTURES THAT WE KNEW WERE ONE OF A KIND. AS WE WERE CAUTIOUSLY

INCHING OUR WAY BACKWARDS SO NOT TO SCARE THIS MAGNIFICENT

BEAST AWAY; TWO YOUNG KIDS CAME RUNNING BY AND GOT EVEN CLOSER

THAN WE DID AND THE ANIMAL NEVER MOVED. GO FIGURE.

ALL IN ALL IT WAS A DAY THAT MET BOTH JACKS AND MY DREAM

EXPECTATIONS. TO THIS DAY I WON'T LET ANYONE SAY THERE IS MORE TO

SEE OUTSIDE OUR COUNTRY. MOST PEOPLE HAVE YET TO SEE WHAT WE

HAVE.

DAY 22—AUGUST 31ST, 1971—TUESDAY

WE SLEPT IN THE PARK AND GOT UP WITH OUR CAMERAS READY AGAIN.

AROUND EVERY CORNER WAS ANOTHER PHOTO OP.

WE HATED TO LEAVE THE PARK. IF IT WASN'T FOR MY LEAK IN THE GAS TANK, I'M SURE WE WOULD HAVE STAYED ANOTHER DAY. HIGHWAY 212 OUT OF YELLOWSTONE PUT US IN LINE TO GO THROUGH BEARTOOTH PASS (10,943 FEET).

ON THE OTHER SIDE WE STOPPED IN RED LODGE, MONTANA AT THE HONDA DEALER AND PATCHED MY TANK AND GOT NEW PLUGS. $8.80 WORTH OF PURE EASE OF MIND! WE COULD NOW RIDE LIKE THE WIND. WIND IT WAS—GOING INTO BILLINGS MONTANA THE WIND WAS PUSHING US BACK AND MAKING IT VERY DIFFICULT TO GO OVER 40 MPH. AS YOU KNOW BY NOW WE DIDN'T HAVE WIND SHIELDS AND THE BIKES DIDN'T HAVE ENOUGH WEIGHT TO CUT THROUGH THE WIND. OUR FACES WERE OKAY

BUT OUR BODIES TURNED INTO A SAIL. THE CONSTANT FORCE ON OUR

CHEST FELT ABOUT 100 LBS.

AT THE I-90 AND I-94 JUNCTION WE CONTINUED ON I-90 BUT THE ROAD

TOOK A TURN AND THE WIND SEEMED TO DROP OFF TO ALMOST NOTHING.

IT WAS LIKE SOMEONE REACHED OVER AND UNPLUGGED THE FAN. WE

WERE NOW IN ROLLING HILLS TYPE OF TERRAIN. LOOKING EAST WE

COULDN'T SEE ANY MAJOR MOUNTAINS FOR THE FIRST TIME IN OUR TRIP.

CUSTER BATTLEFIELD CAME UP ON US QUICK AND PULLING INTO THE

PARK I HAD DOUBTS THAT IT WAS GOING TO BE WORTH THE STOP.

ONCE AGAIN THE VISITORS CENTER OVERWELMED US WITH

INFORMATION. THE BATTLE THAT TOOK PLACE HERE WAS ONE SIDED AND

THE GRAVEYARD SHOWED WERE MOST OF THE SOLDIERS DIED. THE

GRAVESTONES WERE ERECTED AT THE EXACT SPOT THEY FELL. GENERAL

CUSTER WAS RIGHT IN THE MIDDLE OF ALL THESE STONES. OUR NEXT STOP

WAS MILES DOWN THE ROAD AND WE GOT CAUGHT UP IN THE DISPLAYS

AND HISTORY OF THIS SITE AND SPENT MORE TIME THAN WE HAD

EXPECTED.

THE WEATHER WAS DOING WEIRD THINGS, BECAUSE NOW ONLY ONE OR

TWO HOURS SINCE THE HIGH COLD WINDS, WE WERE NOW IN ABOUT 15 TO

20 DEGREE WARMER CLIMATE AND IT WAS STILL. THIS MADE FOR NICE

EASY RIDING ON I-90. SO EASY THAT JACK AND I WERE LAID BACK IN OUR

SEATS RESTING ON OUR GEAR AND WITH OUR FEET UP ON OUR TRAVELING

PEGS. WE MUST HAVE LOOKED VERY COMFORTABLE TO THE THREE THAT

PULLED UP BESIDE US AND OFFERED US A BEER WHILE WE WERE ALL

DRIVING ABOUT 55 TO 60 MPH DOWN THE FREEWAY. THEY GOT A KICK OUT

OF US PULLING UP NEXT TO THEM AND ACCEPTING THE BEER. WE JUST

SLIPPED THEM INTO OUR FIELD JACKET POCKETS AND KEPT RIDING. IF YOU

REMEMBER, THE ADVERTISEMENTS BACK IN THOSE DAYS WAS "YOU'LL

MEET THE NICEST PEOPLE ON A HONDA". WELL WE WERE JUST OUT TO

PLEASE! WHAT CAN I SAY.

WE STOPPED IN GILLETE, WYOMING AND GOT GAS. WE STILL HAD

ANOTHER COUPLE HOURS OF DAYLIGHT BUT NO NEED TO PUSH HARD, THE

NEXT SEVERAL SITES WERE CLOSE BY. WE PURCHASED SOME CANNED

BEANS AND CHOCOLATE MILK TO GO WITH SOME LEFTOVER SANDWICHES AND WE PULLED INTO THE FIRST REST AREA WE SAW.

IT WAS A BEAUTIFUL EVENING. THE SKY WAS CLEAR AND THE TEMPERATURE WAS A LOT WARMER THAN THE NIGHT BEFORE. THE PEOPLE BEFORE US HAD LEFT A LOG IN THE PIT AND A LOT OF COALS ALSO. JACK AND I TALKED A WHILE AND THEN I PLAYED WITH THE RADIO I BROUGHT ALONG. I WAS SURPRISED TO FIND "K-O-M-A" THIS WAS AN OKLAHOMA RADIO STATION THAT MANY SOUTHWEST PEOPLE GREW UP WITH. WE CRAWLED INTO OUR BAGS WITH OUR BELLY'S FULL AND MUSIC IN THE AIR.

CHAPTER 7

DAY 23—SEPTEMBER 1ST, 1971—WEDNESDAY

DEVILS TOWER NATIONAL MONUMENT WAS OUR FIRST STOP THIS GORGOUS MORNING. THIS IS A VERY ODD SHAPED MOUNTAIN THAT JUTS OUT OF THE FLOOR OF THE EARTH. THE INDIAN LEGEND SAYS A BEAR CARVED IT OUT TRYING TO REACH SOME WARRIORS. THAT MUST HAVE BEEN SOME BEAR! WE SAT DOWN AT A PICNIC TABLE AND ATE SOME COOKIES WHICH ATTRACTED SEVERAL LITTLE FRIENDS. THESE LITTLE PRAIRIE DOGS WERE FUN TO WATCH. THEY WERE ABOUT HALF THE SIZE OF THE MARMOTS THAT WE SAW IN MOUNT RAINIER PARK.

WE WERE DISAPPOINTED AT THE NEXT TWO STOPS BECAUSE OUR GOLDEN EAGLE PASS WOULD NOT COVER THE ENTRANCE FEES. **JEWEL CAVE NATIONAL MONUMENT** AND **WIND CAVE NATIONAL MONUMENT** HAD TO BE BYPASSED DUE TO FINANCES. JUST DOWN THE ROAD HOWEVER, A VERY WELL KNOWN SCENIC AREA WAS AWAITING US. **MOUNT RUSHMORE NATIONAL MEMORIAL** IS CLEAR IN EACH AND EVERY ONE OF OUR MINDS. ONCE AGAIN—DON'T ACCEPT WHAT YOU SEE ON T.V. OR IN A MAGAZINE. DON'T RELY ON WHAT YOUR FRIENDS TELL YOU. GO TO ALL THESE PLACES YOURSELF. WORDS AND PICTURES JUST DO NOT DO IT JUSTICE. OUR COUNTRY HAS BUILT A VERY NICE VISITORS CENTER THAT COMPLIMENTS THE AREA AND ASSIST IN THE PATRIOTIC MOOD THAT SURROUNDS THIS MEMORIAL.

BEFORE WE GOT BACK IN THE SADDLES I NOTICED JACK STARING AT HIS MAP AND HE LOOKED UP AND SAID WE COULD EASILY BE AT HIS HOUSE IN FOND-DU-LAC, WISCONSIN SOMETIME TOMORROW! I KNEW THEN THAT JACK WAS READY TO TAKE THE LEAD! HE WAS SNIFFING OUT FAMILIAR GROUNDS AND IT WAS HIS WAY OF SAYING THAT I SHOULD SIT BACK AND LET HIM SHOW ME SOME THINGS OR TWO. NOW TAKE A CLOSE LOOK AT YOUR MAP. I-90 FROM OUR LAST STOP IS ALMOST STRAIGHT AS AN ARROW EAST ALL THE WAY TO OUR NEXT STOP, **<u>PIPESTONE NATIONAL MONUMENT.</u>** IT WAS ALMOST LIKE JACK HAD A MAGNET PULLING HIM HOME, HE WAS OUT FRONT AND THE ONLY THING SLOWING HIM DOWN WAS GAS. SOMEWHERE PAST MITCHELL, SOUTH DAKOTA WE STOPPED AT A REST

AREA TO FINALLY TAKE A BREAK. IT WAS NOW CLOSE TO 11:30 AND WE

HAD PUT 562 MILES ON THE BIKES TODAY. WE ENJOYED OUR SIX PACK.

DAY 24—SEPTEMBER 2ND, 1971—THURSDAY

<u>PIPESTONE NATIONAL MONUMENT</u> WAS VERY INTERESTING TO ME,

JACK HOWEVER STILL HAD THIS MAGNET PULLING AT HIM AND HE WASN'T

ATTRACTED TO THIS SETTING AT ALL. HE TOOK IT IN AND NEVER

COMPLAINED BUT THAT'S AS FAR AS THE ENTHUSIASM WENT. I TRIED TO

DISCUSS THE FACT THAT SOME FAMOUS PIPES HAD STARTED OUT THERE,

BUT ANY SIGN OF PROLONGING THE VISIT WAS OF NO INTEREST TO HIM.

WHEN WE GOT BACK OUT TO THE BIKES WE NOTICED THE CRACK IN HIS

EXHAUST PIPE HAD BECOME LARGER. MY HAIR PIN GAS LEAK HAD

STARTED LEAKING AGAIN AND OTHER MINOR PROBLEMS WERE STARTING

TO SHOW UP. SO—IT WAS TIME TO BECOME MORE AWARE OF OUR BIKES

THAN THE ELEMENTS AROUND US. ABOUT 350 MILES OF CAUTIOUS RIDING

CAN TAKE THE FUN OUT OF RIDING A MOTORCYCLE. IF YOU HAVE EVER

BEEN ON EMPTY AND THE NEXT GAS STATION IS 20 MILES DOWN THE ROAD

AND YOU KNOW IT WILL RUN OUT ANYTIME—THAT'S HOW WE FELT. A

MAJOR BREAKDOWN OR SOMETHING WAS HAUNTING US. IT WAS JUST TO

MUCH FOR US AND WE PULLED OVER AT AROUND 100 MILES FROM FOND-

DU-LAC AND CALLED IT A DAY. EVEN THOUGH THE MAGNET WAS GETTING

STRONGER ON JACK, EVEN HE WAS READY FOR A BREAK. WE STAYED UP

TALKING ABOUT HIS HOME TOWN FOR AN HOUR OR SO. BUT—THAT'S

ANOTHER STORY.

DAY 25—SEPTEMBER 3RD, 1971—FRIDAY

WE GOT INTO FOND-DU-LAC, WISCONSIN AT 9 AM ON A FRIDAY MORNING

AND DID NOT LEAVE UNTIL THE NEXT WEDNESDAY MORNING. CALL IT

SEVENTH INNING STRETCH OR THE HALF TIME OR WHAT EVER—WE NEEDED

A BREAK!!

THE DAYS WERE FILLED WITH FIXING OUR BIKES AND THE NIGHTS WERE A LITTLE OF EVERYTHING. I REMEMBER A PLACE CALLED "HIPPO'S", THERE WERE MORE GIRLS THAN GUYS. WE ALSO CHASED COP CARS, AND PLAYED POKER TILL WEE HOURS IN THE MORNINGS. JUST ONE PARTY AFTER ANOTHER. BUT—THAT'S ANOTHER STORY.

JACK'S MOTHER WAS FABULOUS-SHE COOKED, TOOK CARE OF THE LAUNDRY AND JUST MADE OUR STAY VERY RELAXING. EACH INSTANCE IS A STORY IN ITSELF AND THE LOCAL NEWSPAPER EVEN SENT OUT A CUTE LITTLE THING TO INTERVIEW US AND YOU CAN READ THE ARTICLE IN THE BACK OF THIS BOOK.

DAY 30—SEPTEMBER 8TH, 1971—WEDNESDAY

WE WERE BOTH RESTED, CLEANED AND FIXED UP; INCLUDING OUR

BIKES! IT WAS TIME TO SAY GOODBYE TO ALL THE GREAT PEOPLE OF FOND-

DU- LAC.

<u>*CHAPTER 8*</u>

DAY 30—SEPTEMBER 8TH, 1971—WEDNESDAY

WE STARTED LATER THAN WE WANTED TO BECAUSE MRS. KRAMER MADE ANOTHER BREAKFAST THAT WAS VERY DIFFICULT TO SAY NO TO. SHE EVEN MADE SANDWICHES AND FRUIT FOR US TO TAKE ALONG. THANK YOU MRS. KRAMER!

FROM FOND-DU-LAC IT WAS AN EASY RIDE DOWN TO CHICAGO AND THE TALL BUILDINGS WERE VERY IMPRESSIVE TO THIS COWBOY. WHAT WASN'T WAS THE TRAFFIC. JACK LATER TOLD ME THAT WE WERE LUCKY BECAUSE WE DIDN'T HIT THE RUSH HOUR. IT TURNED OUT TO BE GOOD TRAINING HOWEVER; THE WHOLE EAST COAST IS CROWDED TO MY EYES. WE PUSHED ON TO DETROIT SO WE MIGHT HAVE A CHANCE TO SEE SOME AUTO FACTORIES AT FULL SHIFT. ON I-94 WE GOT ANOTHER GROUP PULL UP BESIDE US AND PASS MORE LIQUID REFRESHMENTS TO US. IT MUST HAVE BEEN OUR BEARDS OR SOMETHING BECAUSE EVERYONE STARTED BECOMING MORE AND MORE INTERESTED IN US.

WHEN WE GOT TO THE CANADIAN BORDER WE HAD TO PAY A TOLL OF $.35 FOR MOTORCYCLES. THE AMBASSADOR BRIDGE WAS NEAT BUT IT ERASED A VERY LONG MYTH THAT I HAD HAD SINCE A LITTLE BOY. SINCE I HAD LIVED IN THE SOUTHWEST ALMOST MY WHOLE LIFE, I BELIEVED THAT AS SOON AS YOU CROSSED INTO CANADA IT WOULD BE "WHITE"—YOU KNOW—SNOW! I KNOW, THAT IS SILLY, BUT WE ALL HAVE THOSE

MISCONCEPTIONS. JACK'S WAS THAT THERE WOULD BE BEARS RUNNING ALL OVER YELLOWSTONE PARK! HIS HEART WOULD HAVE BEEN BROKEN IF WE WOULDN'T HAVE SEEN THAT ONE. MY HEART, ON THE OTHER HAND, DIDN'T MIND AT ALL THAT THERE WAS NO SNOW ON THE GROUND. WE WERE NOW IN ANOTHER COUNTRY AND THE SUN WAS DOWN OVER AN HOUR AGO. WE CAMPED OUT ABOUT 15 MILES THIS SIDE OF WOODSTOCK, CANADA. THE ROAD SIDE CAMP GROUNDS WERE ABOUT ONE THIRD FILLED AND IT WAS SO LATE WE DIDN'T HAVE TO PAY A FEE. JACK AND I STAYED UP A WHILE TALKING ABOUT HIS FRIENDS AND THE PARTIES THAT TOOK PLACE JUST A FEW NIGHTS BEFORE.

DAY 31—SEPTEMBER 9TH, 1971—THURSDAY

THE MORNING AIR WAS PURE AND STILL. JACK CHECKED THE MAP AND NOTED WE WERE CLOSE TO OUR NEXT STOP. WE COULD TAKE OUR TIME AND LEISURELY ENJOY THE SURROUNDING FOR A CHANGE. THERE WAS SOMETHING ABOUT BEING IN ANOTHER COUNTRY THAT SLOWED US DOWN A BIT.

WE GOT TO **NIAGARA FALLS** AROUND 10 A.M. WHICH PUT US IN THE

THICK OF THE TOURIST. WE JUST BLENDED IN AND TOOK OUR FAVORITE

PICTURES. ONCE AGAIN WE WERE STANDING AT ANOTHER NATURAL

WONDER IN AWE OF THE BEAUTY. THE RAINBOWS THAT ARE CREATED BY THE MIST OF THE FALLS ARE A PUNCTUATION TO THE ENDLESS ADJECTIVES ONE CAN LIST TO DISCRIBE THIS AREA. IT IS NOT A SURPRISE THAT SO MANY COME SO FAR TO WITNESS THIS ACTIVE CARVING OR SCULPTURING OF OUR LAND. ONCE AGAIN PICTURES DO NOT DO IT JUSTICE. YOU HAVE TO BE THERE TO APPRECIATE IT! WE DID INTRODUCE OURSELVES TO A NEW FRIEND. WHEN WE SAT DOWN TO ENJOY SOME SANDWICHES AND ITEMS MRS. KRAMER MADE FOR US, JACK ROLLED UP A PIECE OF FOIL WITH FOOD INSIDE AND WE HAD INTERTAINMENT FOR THE NEXT 5 MINUTES. WHEN THE CHIPMUNK GOT TO THE CENTER OF THE FOIL, HE WAS NOT AMUSED TO FIND A SMALL PIECE OF BREAD. HE THEN GAVE JACK A DIRTY STARE! SECONDS LATER WE WERE GIVING IT WHATEVER IT WANTED. WE DIDN'T KNOW HOW MANY FRIENDS IT HAD SO WE PLAYED IT SAFE, AND TRIED TO STAY ON IT'S GOOD SIDE. WE HEADED OUT OF BUFFALO, NEW YORK ON HIGHWAY 20. THIS ROAD HIT A LOT OF SMALL TOWNS AND WE STAYED AWAY FROM THE BIG RIGS ON THE FREEWAY. GOING SLOW ON THE CURVES AND SPEEDING UP TO 50 MPH OR SO ON THE STRAIGHTS WAS WHAT THE WHOLE DAY WAS LIKE. IN AND OUT OF SMALL TOWNS AND STOPPING FOR GAS HERE AND THERE. AT OUR LAST STOP WE PICKED UP SOME CHOCOLATE MILK AGAIN AND SOME WIENERS IN A CAN (THOSE SMALL ONES). IT WAS TIME TO PICK A SPOT FOR TONIGHT AND JUST AROUND THE CURVE WE SAW A SIGN THAT SAID "WILD LIFE REFUGE" 1 MILE AHEAD.

WE TOOK THAT AS AN INVITATION TO ANOTHER PARTY AND PULLED INTO AN OPEN AREA. LATER THAT NIGHT WE GOT ATTACKED BY THOUSANDS OF LITTLE FLYING BUGS. THAT WAS THE ONLY WILD LIFE WE SAW.

DAY 32—SEPTEMBER 10TH, 1971—FRIDAY

IT WAS WET AGAIN! THE FOG HAD ROLLED IN OVER NIGHT AND COVERED EVERYTHING. MY BUBBLE SHIELD FOR MY HELMET WASN'T GOING TO DO ANYGOOD TODAY SO I PACKED IT UP AND STARTED TO RIDE. THE FOG WAS SO THICK IT MIGHT AS WELL HAVE BEEN RAINING. THE WATER WAS ONCE AGAIN FINDING ITSELF DOWN MY FIELD JACKET AND UNDER MY LEATHER SHIRT AND IT DIDN'T STOP THERE. THE AREA WAS GREEN AND IN OTHER CIRCUMSTANCES WOULD HAVE BEEN FAVORABLE TO PICTURES. WHEN WE GOT TO ALBANY, NEW YORK WE JUST HAD TO STOP AT A COFFEE SHOP FOR A CUP AND A DONUT. WE GOT A LOT OF STARES AT THE SHOP AND NO ONE TALKED WITH US. THE VISIBILITY IMPROVED OVER THE NEXT 20 MINUTES OR SO AND AWAY WE WENT. ABOUT 15 MILES DOWN THE ROAD A NY POLICE CAR STOPPED US FOR WHAT HE SAID WAS A NORMAL CHECK. WE HAD JUST BEEN HALF WAY AROUND THE UNITED STATES AND THIS GUY WANTED TO CHECK OUR REGISTRATIONS. HE MUST HAVE BEEN TRYING TO IMPRESS HIMSELF BECAUSE HE WASN'T IMPRESSING US. HIS COMMENT WAS HE THOUGHT THE BIKES MIGHT HAVE BEEN STOLEN. (MY PLATES WERE TEXAS AND JACKS WERE WISCONSIN).

WE STAYED ON 20 AND AS THE DAY WENT ON THE FOG LIFTED AND THE ROAD WAS BEAUTIFUL. LOT'S OF GREENERY! WE PULLED INTO INDIAN ORCHARDS, MASSACHUSETTS AROUND 4 P.M. A ARMY BUDDY OF OURS BEGGED US TO CALL HIM WHEN WE ARRIVED AND HE WOULD PUT US UP FOR A NIGHT. WELL, HE WAS NOWHERE TO BE FOUND.

AFTER A WHOLE DAY OF FIGHTING BUGS, FOG, COPS AND JUST KNOWING A HOT SHOWER WAS WAITING FOR US; IT WAS HARD TO ACCEPT HIS MOTHERS REPLY THAT SHE HAD NO WAY OF GETTING IN TOUCH WITH HIM. I UNDERSTOOD WHEN THE MOTHERS WERE PROTECTING THEIR KIDS IN DISNEYLAND BUT THIS GUY WAS IN THE ARMY WITH US. OH WELL, THAT'S ANOTHER STORY…

WE STOPPED AT A CONVIENCE STORE AND GOT SOME CAN GOODS AND STARTED LOOKING FOR A PLACE TO SLEEP. WE PULLED UP TO A REST AREA AND THERE WAS A NAVY GUY ON HIS WAY TO MAINE. HE WAS HITCHHIKING AND STAYED AND TALKED WITH US. WE DRANK BEER, ATE SPAGETTI, SANDWICH AND A FEW COOKIES (SO MY JOURNAL SAYS). THE GUY CAUGHT A RIDE BEFORE WE BEDDED DOWN.

DAY 33—SEPTEMBER 11TH, 1971—SATURDAY

IT WASN'T COLD AT ALL THIS MORNING. THE FOG WAS STILL IN THOUGH AND THAT MADE FOR SLOW DRIVING AND VERY MOIST AIR. THIS WAS BECOMING OLD HAT TO US BY NOW AND WE WERE LEARNING TO LIVE WITH

THE ELEMENTS. WE GOT TO CONCORD, MASSACHUSETTS AND WENT

STRAIGHT TO **NORTH BRIDGE** AND THE **MINUTE MEN MONUMENT**.

WE WERE REALLY GETTING DEEP INTO OUR HISTORY BOOKS NOW AND

JACK AND I WERE READING EVERY WORD ON EVERY STATUE. TO WALK

WHERE THESE MEN WALKED AND TO WATCH THE PRESENTATIONS AT THE

VISITORS STATION BROUGHT MEANING TO ALL THOSE TEST IN GRADE

SCHOOL. I MEAN, HERE WE WERE, STANDING WHERE THE "FIRST SHOT THAT

WAS HEARD AROUND THE WORLD".

WE THEN PASSED UP BOSTON TO HURRY TO **PLYMOUTH ROCK.**

SCAVENGERS AND SOUVENIR HUNTERS OVER THE YEARS DWENDLED THE POOR THING DOWN TO A MEAR BOULDER BEFORE THEY PLACED THIS BUILDING AROUND IT. LOOKING OUT INTO CAP COD BAY YOU COULD IMAGINE THE CLIPPER SHIPS ARRIVING FOR THE FIRST TIME. IT WAS EVEN EASIER TO IMAGINE AFTER OUR NEXT STOP AT THE REPLICA OF THE **"MAYFLOWER"**. THIS SHIP WAS GORGOUS IN IT'S COLORS AND WELL KEPT WOODEN MASK AND HULL. THIS IS THE ONLY WAY TO STUDY HISTORY.

AS THE PICTURE SHOWS IT WAS GETTING DUSK AND WE CALLED A

FRIEND OF MY FUTURE MOTHER-IN-LAW. THEY ALSO HAD OFFERED TO LET

US STOP IN FOR A NIGHT OR SO. THE PERRY'S WERE MOST GRACIOUS AND

THEIR BIG WHITE DOG WAS - - WELLLL, YOU KNOW - - BIG!

DAY 34—SEPTEMBER 12TH, 1971—SUNDAY

BREAKFAST WAS UNBELIEVABLE! THE PERRY'S HAD SPENT THE

EVENING SHOWING US FILMS AND DRINKING BEER WITH US AND SHARING

EVERYTHING THEY COULD. AND NOW, SHE WAS GOING ALL OUT TO MAKE

OUR STAY MEMORABLE. EGGS, BACON, HASH, POTATOES, JUICE—YOU

NAME IT AND IT WAS ON THE TABLE. SHE SAID IT WAS IN PAYMENT FOR

THE SHARING OF OUR ADVENTURES THE NIGHT BEFORE. I NOTICE THEY

BOTH WISHED THEY WERE 25 YEARS YOUNGER AND OUT WITH US. SHE

TOPPED EVERYTHING OFF BY FIXING SANDWICHES AND FILLING OUR BAGS

WITH GOODIES.

WE HEADED OUT OF PROVIDENCE, RHODE ISLAND ON HOPES OF MAKING NEW YORK, CITY TODAY. AS WE LEFT THE PERRY'S THEY SAID WE HAD A NORMAL BEAUTIFUL DAY OF WEATHER AHEAD OF US.

THE SKY WAS A THICK GRAY WITH VERY LOW CLOUDS. IT WASN'T FOG, JUST A VERY LOW CLOUD COVER. DOWN THE ROAD A BIT IT STARTED TO DRIZZLE. NOT A STORM LIKE WE KNOW IN THE SOUTHWEST BUT MORE OF A WEATHER FRONT THAT MOVES SLOWLY IN. WE PUT OUR EXTRA GEAR ON AND HOPED FOR THE BEST. WE KNEW WE WERE RIGHT ON THE EDGE OF THIS WEATHER FRONT BECAUSE WE WERE GOING IN AND OUT OF THE RAIN. WHEN WE GOT TO OUR NEXT STOP WE HAD BROKEN OUT OF THE RAIN AND IT GAVE US A BREAK. THE ***MYSTIC SEA PORT*** WAS ON THE ATLANTIC SHORE LINE WHICH SEEMED TO BE PROTECTED BY THE FRONT. THIS SPOT HAS SEVERAL OLD CLIPPER SHIPS AND LOTS OF BOARD WALK ATTRACTIONS. THE PICTURE OF ONE OF THE SHIPS ALSO SHOWS THE LOW CLOUD COVER BEHIND US. I MADE A PHONE CALL TO OUR NEXT STOP IN CARMEL, NY AND SHE WAS NOW MARRIED. THAT'S ANOTHER STORY…

WHEN WE GOT TO WEST POINT THE RAIN WAS NOW STEADY. NO PICTURES COULD BE TAKEN AND OUR STAY WAS SHORTENED BY THE WEATHER. IT SEEMED LIKE WE WERE DOOMED TO A BAD DAY. THERE WAS NO WIND AT ALL AND THE RAIN JUST WOULDN'T STOP. JACK WAS MORE AWARE OF THE WEATHER PATTERN THAN I AND HE SAID THIS COULD GO ON FOR DAYS. BEING A SUNSHINE TYPE OF GUY, IT WASN'T MAKING ME HAPPY AT ALL.

I CONVINCED JACK TO STOP IN THE NEXT OPEN FIELD AND MAKE CAMP.

IT WAS ONLY ABOUT 4 P.M. AND WE HAD PLENTY OF TIME TO PUT MORE MILES BEHIND US, I JUST COULDN'T. WE PARKED OUR BIKES NEXT TO EACH OTHER AND BUILD A SHELTER OF SORTS OUT OF OUR GEAR AND BRANCHES THAT WAS LYING ON THE GROUND. WE DID WHAT WE COULD TO KEEP OURSELVES DRY AND HALFWAY COMFORTABLE. THE RAIN WOULD INCREASE AND DIE DOWN AND INCREASE AGAIN FOR THE NEXT SEVERAL HOURS. THEN THE SUN WENT DOWN. ALL THE BUGS IN THE WORLD MUST HAVE HEARD THE DINNER BELL. IT WAS PITCH DARK, RAINING AND NOW WE HAD ALL KINDS OF THINGS CRAWLING ALL OVER US. JACK HAD A SMALL FLASHLIGHT AN THE GROUND WAS CRAWLING WITH LIFE. I REACHED UP AND TURNED MY HEADLIGHT ON AND EVEN THOUGH IT WAS

RAINING THE REFLECTIONS WERE FLYING AROUND AS WELL AS DROPPING

TO THE GROUND, AND THE RATIO WAS ABOUT 2 TO 1 ON THE ITEMS FLYING

AROUND VERSUS THE RAIN FALLING DOWN. WE KNEW THIS WASN'T A

PLACE TO BE TONIGHT.

WE PACKED UP AND HEADED TO NEW YORK, CITY. THE PICTURES WERE

TERRIBLE AND THE NIGHT WAS JUST AS BAD. BUT, WE MISSED THE RUSH

HOURS AND THE CROWDS.

DAY 35—SEPTEMBER 13TH, 1971—MONDAY

IT WAS NOW 5 AM AND WE HAD MADE IT THROUGH THE METROPLEX OF

NEW YORK AND I DECIDED IT WAS MY TURN TO BUY BREAKFAST. THE

TOTAL FOR BOTH OF US WAS $3.00 AND OUR BELLIES WERE FULL. WE WERE

NOW TIRED AND STILL VERY WET AND IT WAS STILL RAINING. NOTHING TO

DO BUT RIDE.

OUR NEXT STOP WAS **"MORRISTOWN NATIONAL HISTORICAL SITE"**.

WHEN WE ARRIVED IT WAS STILL RAINING AND WE MUST HAVE LOOKED

PITIFUL. THE RANGER WAS ONLY A FEW YEARS OLDER THAN US AND WE

HIT IT OFF WITH EACH OTHER. HE SAID THAT MOST OF THE TRAFFIC TO THE

SITE WAS NOW OVER AND HE DIDN'T EXPECT ANYONE UNTIL THE

WEEKEND. HE THEN OFFERED HIS GARAGE FOR US TO GET DRY IN AND

WAIT OUT THE RAIN. JACK AND I WERE VERY THANKFUL. THE RAIN HAD

SOAKED ALL THE WAY THROUGH OUR CLOTHS AND IT WAS NOW

DAMPERING OUR ATTITUDES. THE RANGER TOOK OUR FIELD JACKETS AND

SHIRTS AND THROUGH THEM IN THE DRYER FOR US. JACK AND I THEN TOOK

A WELL DESERVED NAP. I WOKE UP AT 3 P.M. AND IT WAS STILL RAINING SO

I CONKED OUT AGAIN. THE RANGER CAME IN AT AROUND 7 P.M. AND SAID

THE NEWS SHOWS THE RAIN TO QUIT SOMETIME IN THE MORNING. HE THEN

OFFERED US TO STAY THE NIGHT. THIS SHOULD NOT HAVE SURPRISED US BY NOW; AFTER THE CONTINUED FRIENDLINESS AND HOSPITALITY THAT EVERYONE HAD SHOWN.

WE OPENED UP A CAN OF BEANS AND ATE SANDWICHES AND DRANK SOME POP THE RANGER BROUGHT IN FOR US. WE ALSO TOOK THE OPPORTUNITY TO TIGHTEN UP OUR CHAINS AND DO SOME PLANNING FOR THE NEXT SEVERAL DAYS AHEAD OF US.

CHAPTER 9

DAY 36—SEPTEMBER 14TH, 1971—TUESDAY

BOY—WHAT A DIFFERENCE A DAY MAKES! WE WOKE UP AN IT WASN'T RAINING. OUR CLOTHS WERE DRY. THE BIKES WERE TIGHTENED UP. WE HAD ALL THE SLEEP WE COULD TAKE AND NOW IT WAS RIDING TIME!

PHILADELPHIA WAS PICKED AS A DISTINATION BECAUSE OF THE OVERWHELMING HISTORY THAT SURROUND THIS GREAT CITY. WE STOPPED AT SEVERAL SITES, INCLUDING THE LIBERTY BELL AND INDEPENDENCE HALL.

THE RAIN HAD STOPPED BUT THE CLOUD COVER WAS DROPPING ONCE

AGAIN. THE TRAFFIC AND CROWDS AT THE SITES WERE DOWN DUE TO OUR

MID-WEEK VISIT. THE SMALLER CROWDS DID GIVE US THE CHANCE TO

VIEW SEVERAL FILMS AND PRESENTATIONS AT EACH VISITORS STATIONS.

HISTORY IS EVERYWHERE IN THIS TOWN. WE PUSHED ON TO **"GETTYSBURG**

<u>**NATIONAL MONUMENT"**</u> WHICH ADDED TO THE DAYS HISTORY LESSON.
WE WERE QUICKLY NOTING THAT THE WESTERN UNITED STATES WAS
MOSTLY NATURAL WONDERS; THE EASTERN PART WAS ALL HISTORY. WE
ALSO WEREN'T PUTTING AS MANY MILES ON THE BIKES BETWEEN SITES.
AROUND EVERY CORNER WAS ANOTHER BATTLEFIELD OR CAPITAL
BUILDING WITH A HISTORICAL PAST. AT CATOCTIN MOUNTAIN PARK JUST
BEFORE FREDERICK WE CALLED IT A DAY AND BOUGHT TWO SIX PACKS
AND ATE SANDWICHES OF MUSTARD, CHEESE AND SALOMIE SLICES. THE
BEER WAS $1.45 AND THE REST WAS $.39.

DAY 37—SEPTEMBER 15TH, 1971—WEDNESDAY

WE WOKE UP TO CLEAR SKY BUT SINCE WE STAYED IN A MOUNTAIN
PARK THE DEW WAS HEAVY. WE KNEW THAT ONCE THE SUN CAME UP AND
WE WERE DOWN THE MOUNTAIN THAT WOULD ALL BE GONE.

WE GASED UP IN FREDERICK ($.75 FOR ME) AND THEN HEADED TO
<u>**"HARPERS FERRY NATIONAL MONUMENT"**</u>. OUR HISTORY LESSONS
CONTINUED WITH VIDEOS AND MUSEUMS. THIS IS A SMALL TOWN THAT

BECOMES SWAMPED WITH VISITORS OVER THE WEEKENDS. TODAY WE HAD

ALL THE ATTENTION OF EVERY VENDOR IN THE TOWN. THAT MIGHT HAVE

BEEN THE WAY WE WERE DRESSED AND LOOKED BUT ALSO BECAUSE IT

WAS MID-WEEK. JACK AND I WAS CASUALLY TAKING IN THE AREA

BECAUSE OF THE FALL COLORS IN THE MOUNTAIN TERRAIN. THE LEAVES

WERE TURNING COLORS AND A NICE BREEZE WAS DROPPING THEM ONE BY

ONE. THIS MADE FOR AN EVEN GREATER MOMENT WHEN WE REACHED THE

VIEWING POINT WHERE THE POTOMAC RIVER AND SHENANDOAH RIVER

MEET. JACK PARTICULLARLY TOOK PLEASURE IN THIS SPOT. THE WOODS

NEAR HERE ARE THICK AND THE ROLLING MOUNTAINS ARE ALL

ACCOMPANIED BY A STREAM OR RIVER NESTLED AT THERE BASE. IT TOOK

SOME COAXING TO BRING JACK DOWN FROM THIS SPOT AND IT WASN'T ME

WHO DID IT—SHE WAS JUST VISITING THE SIGHTS LIKE WE WERE

AND…WELL, THAT'S ANOTHER STORY.

I DRUG JACK BACK TO HIS BIKE AND AWAY TO **WASHINGTON D.C.** WE

WENT. NOW, I KNOW, WE SAID THAT BUILDINGS AND CITIES WEREN'T THE

PURPOSE OF THIS TRIP BUT COME ON—THIS IS OUR CAPITOL!!

WE SAW EVERY SITE. WE DROVE EVERY STREET. WE LISTENED TO

COUNTLESS PRESENTATIONS; INSIDE THE BUILDINGS AS WELL AS OUTSIDE.

THE WEATHER WAS PERFECT. THE DAY WAS GREAT.

JACK AND I WERE COUNTING OUR BLESSING AND NO LONGER WONDERING WHY WE SPENT YEARS IN THE SERVICE TO PROTECT THIS NATION. "WE DID WHAT WE DID BECAUSE WE KNEW WE HAD TO" WAS A FAVORITE SAYING AROUND US OVER THE YEARS; IT WAS ONLY NOW THAT IT SUNK HOME. THIS IS A PROUD NATION AND WE WERE PROUD TO HAVE SERVED IT. OUR FIELD JACKETS HAD NEVER BEEN WORN CLOSER TO OUR HEARTS THAN WHEN WE GOT TO THE **"THE TOMB OF THE UNKNOWN SOLDIERS"** AND THE ETERNAL FLAME FOR JOHN F. KENNEDY.

WITH LOTS OF DAYLIGHT LEFT WE HEADED TOWARDS OUR NEXT STOP. **"SHANANDOAH NATIONAL PARK"** IS BEAUTIFUL! IT MIGHT HAVE BEEN

THE MOOD I WAS IN, OR JUST THE PLAIN BEAUTY. THE TRANQUILITY OF THE

SUNSET WAS PICTURE PERFECT TO END THIS DAY.

DAY 38—SEPTEMBER 16TH, 1971—THURSDAY

    THE BEER AND THE HOURS OF TALK LAST NIGHT PUT US IN A FABULOUS

MOOD THIS MORNING. FROM MY SLEEPING BAG I SAW A TURTLE CALMLY

MAKING HIS WAY ACROSS THE AREA WE WERE IN. JACK WAS STILL

SNORING AWAY AND THE COLD AIR CAUSED MY BREATH TO FORM DURING

EVERY EXHALE. I WOULD USUALLY HOP UP AND GIVE JACK A NUDGE AND

THE DAY WOULD START. TODAY, I GAVE HIM ANOTHER 10 MINUTES OR SO—

WHAT A NICE GUY.

ONCE UP AND RIDING THE SCENERY WAS GREAT. THIS WAS PERFECT MOTORCYCLE RIDING COUNTRY. WINDING ROADS, MOUNTAINOUS, COOL AIR AND LOTS OF DAYLIGHT AHEAD OF US—SO I STOPPED! JACK KEPT GOING! BOY WAS HE MAD! HE WAS DAYDREAMING ALSO AND MUST HAVE GONE A FEW MILES BEFORE HE NOTICED I WAS NO WHERE IN SIGHT. I TOLD HIM I JUST HAD TO GET A PICTURE OF THE ROAD TO REMEMBER IT AND HE KNEW I WAS CRAZY THEN. WE PROMISED TO SIGNAL EACH OTHER FROM THEN ON. WE DROVE OUT OF THAT PARK AND RIGHT INTO THE NEXT "**<u>BLUE RIDGE PARKWAY</u>**", WHICH ACTUALLY RUNS ALL THE WAY DOWN INTO GEORGIA. WE MADE A LEFT TURN AT BIG ISLAND, VIRGINIA.

OUR NEXT STOP WAS **"APPOMATTOX COURT HOUSE NATIONAL PARK"**
THE GRAVE YARD OF THE LAST 19 PEOPLE WHO DIED IN THE CIVIL WAR AND
THE HOUSE (NOT THE COURT HOUSE, WHICH WAS NEXT DOOR) WHERE THE
SURRENDER OF THE CONFEDERATE ARMY TOOK PLACE WAS THE FOCAL
POINTS OF THIS STOP. ALL OF THE PARKS AND MONUMENTS THAT WE
STOPPED AT WERE WELL GROOMED AND MAINTAINED; THIS PARK WAS
ALSO.

THAT EVENING WE SLEPT AT A ROAD SIDE PARK NEAR SALISBURY,
NORTH CAROLINA. WE SPURGED A LITTLE AND GOT SOME BEEF STEW WITH
OUR BEER. I WAS KEEPING TABS ON MY EXPENSES AND I FELT MORE AND
MORE COMFORTABLE THAT I HAD ENOUGH TO MAKE IT BACK TO EL PASO,
TEXAS. WE EVEN STARTED BUYING PIES AND COOKIES.

<u>*CHAPTER 10*</u>

DAY 39 OF 53—SEPTEMBER 17TH, 1971—FRIDAY

WE WERE NOW OVER TWO THIRDS OF THE WAY AROUND THE U.S.A. OUR BEARDS WERE DARK AND OUR LEATHERS HAD BECOME PART OF US. THE DAILY ROUTINE WAS MORE THAN TOLERABLE, IT WAS DOWN RIGHT FANTASTIC. WE HAD SOME INCONVENIENCES BUT THE REWARDS WERE PLENTY. TODAY WOULD BE A DAY OF JUST PURE RIDING. THERE WAS NO SPECIAL SPOT ON THE MAP MARKED OFF FOR US TO STOP AT, JUST THE OPEN ROAD. SO WE JUST STARTED CLICKING OFF THE MILES; CHARLOTTE, NORTH CAROLINA; COLUMBIA, SOUTH CAROLINA; AUGUSTA, GEORGIA FINALLY OUR LAST GAS STOP OF THE DAY WAS STATESBORO, GEORGIA. NOW THAT'S RIDING. 414 MILES, THREE STATES AND A LOT OF BUGS ON OUR FACE SHIELDS. THE BUGS GOT REALLY BAD AGAIN THAT NIGHT AND WE DROVE BACK INTO TOWN AND GOT SOME GULF INSECT REPELLENT ($.50). IT WORKED WONDERS. THEY WOULD FLY ALL AROUND US BUT WOULD NOT LAND. DURING DINNER IT STARTED RAINING BUT STOPPED BEFORE WE FINISHED. SOMETIME DURING THE NIGHT IT RAINED AGAIN.

DAY 40—SEPTEMBER 18TH, 1971—SATURDAY

THE NIGHT WASN'T THAT PLEASANT SO NEITHER ONE OF US HAD A HARD TIME LEAVING THE INCOMPLETE REST AREA. IT WAS OFF THE ROAD AND IT HAD PICNIC TABLES BUT THE RESTROOMS AND FACILITIES WERE NOT

FINISHED. BESIDES, WE WERE HEADING TOWARDS A WARMER CLIMATE.

WHEN WE GOT TO **<u>CASTILLO DE SAN MARCOS NATIONAL MONUMENT</u>**

THE VISITORS CENTER SHOWED US VARIOUS FORTS ALONG THE ATLANTIC

COAST. THIS WAS SOMEWHAT OF A RELIEF BECAUSE JACK AND I HAD

CHANGED THE ROUTE A LITTLE AND WE HAD MISSED SEVERAL FORTS TO

THE NORTH. THE EDUCATIONAL FILMS WE SAW WOULD MENTION AND

EVEN PICTURE THESE ALONG WITH THE ONE WE WERE AT. WALKING

AROUND THE GROUNDS IT WAS EASY TO IMAGINE THE ACTIVITY THAT

WENT ON DURING A SKIRMISH. IT BECAME EVEN MORE CLEAR WHEN WE

SAW THE NEXT FORT ABOUT 15 MILES DOWN THE ROAD. **<u>FORT</u>**

<u>MONTONZA</u> WAS A LOOKOUT POST.

"THE JOHN F. KENNEDY SPACE CENTER" WAS NOT ON MY LIST BUT WE

JUST HAD TO STOP. ONCE AGAIN WE WERE IMPRESSED BY WHAT THE

PUBLIC COULD SEE FOR FREE. THE VISITOR CENTER EVEN GAVE US TIPS ON

WHAT TO SEE DOWN THE ROAD AND WHICH BEACHES WERE OPEN AND HAD

FREE FACILITIES.

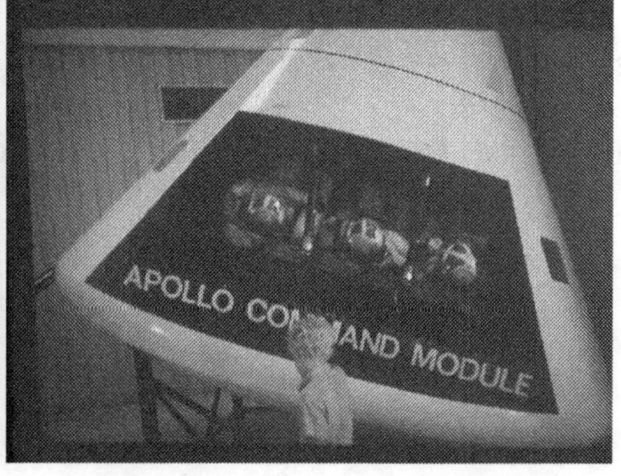

THEY DIDN'T HAVE TO TELL US TWICE. WE JUMPED ON OUR BIKES AND GOT TO ONE AS QUICK AS POSSIBLE. THE ONE WE PICKED DIDN'T HAVE A NAME POSTED BUT THE SHOWERS WERE WORKING AND THE SAND WAS WHITE. THAT'S ALL IT TOOK TO PUT SOME GRINS ON OUR FACES. AFTER TAKING ONE SHOWER AND THEN SWIMMING IN THE OCEAN FOR AN HOUR WE TOOK ANOTHER SHOWER TO GET THE SALT OFF. TWO SHOWERS IN ONE DAY—WOW—WE COULD GO FOR WEEKS NOW! WE WERE CLEANED UP AND EVEN FELT HUMAN ENOUGH TO STRIKE UP A CONVERSATION WITH A FEW GIRLS ON THE BEACH…BUT, THAT'S ANOTHER STORY. THE EVENING WAS FANTASTIC! THE SOUND OF WAVES COMING IN AND BIRDS FLYING OVER WAS ALL THAT WAS NECESSARY FOR A DEEP SLEEP.

DAY 41—SEPTEMBER 19TH, 1971—SUNDAY

AT OUR FIRST GAS STOP WE ALSO CHANGED OIL AND HAD BREAKFAST. WE THEN SLOWLY ROAD SOUTH DOWN HIGHWAY 1 STOPPING AT ALMOST EACH AND EVERY BEACH. WE BOTH SAID THE VIEW OF THE OCEAN KEPT PULLING US IN BUT THE REAL REASON WAS THE CHICKS. THEY WERE EVERYWHERE. IT WAS SUNDAY AND ONLY 8:30 A.M. AND THE BEACHES WERE FILLING UP. WHEN WE PULLED INTO MIAMI IT GOT EVEN BETTER.

THE WEATHER WAS GREAT AND WARM ENOUGH THAT EVERYONE WAS

RUNNING AROUND IN ALMOST NOTHING. WE COULDN'T TELL IF THEY WERE

TOURIST OR LOCALS AND REALLY DIDN'T CARE. THEY WERE FRIENDLY

THOUGH. IT WAS AT THAT MOMENT JACK AND I MADE A FARE JUDGEMENT

CALL. WE EITHER WENT DOWN TO KEY WEST, A ROUND TRIP OF 250 MILES,

OR GET LUNCH AND TALK WITH THE LOCALS. LUNCH WAS GOOD AND THE

LOCALS WERE BETTER…BUT—YOU KNOW THE REST, THAT'S ANOTHER

STORY.

THE **<u>"EVERGLADES NATIONAL PARK"</u>** WAS VISITED BY US AT THE WRONG TIME. THAT IS WHAT THE GUIDE TOLD US. THE WILDLIFE WAS NOT OUT AS MUCH NOW AND THE UPCOMING FRONT WAS CAUSING THEM TO DIG IN ALSO. THE SKY WAS GETTING DARK AND AWAY WE WENT. IT WAS AROUND 7 PM WHEN WE DECIDED TO GET OUR FIRST MOTEL ROOM ($4.70). THIS WAS UNACCEPTABLE DURING THE MANY HOURS OF PLANNING THIS TRIP. HOWEVER, WE WERE COVERED IN SALT, SAND AND BLACK BUGS. I WAS READY TO MAKE AN EXCEPTION. WE NOW HAD A TELEVISION AND COULD SETTLE IN FOR A NICE EVENING BUT WITHOUT BEER! IT WAS SUNDAY AND BEER COULD NOT BE SOLD. OH WELL, THE BEDS WERE SOFT.

DAY 42—SEPTEMBER 20TH, 1971—MONDAY

WE TOOK FULL ADVANTAGE OF THE ROOM WITH YET ANOTHER SHOWER AND A LATE START OF AROUND 10 A.M. WHICH HAPPENED TO BE CHECK OUT TIME. THE TOWEL GIRL BROUGHT US SOME ORANGE JUICE TO GIVE US A FAREWELL DRINK. SUCH FRIENDLY PEOPLE!

WHEN WE PULLED INTO SARASOTA, FLORIDA JACK SPOTTED AN 'ALL YOU CAN EAT' SIGN FOR ONLY $1.39 EACH. WE STUFFED OURSELVES AND THEN ROAD ON. WE WERE CRUISING DOWN THE ROAD WHEN JACK NOTICED MY REAR TIRE. WE PULLED OVER AND TOOK A PICTURE THAT SHOWED THE CORDS OF THE TIRE COMING THROUGH. WE STOPPED AT LAKE CITY,

FLORIDA AND GOT GROCERIES FOR THE NIGHT AND MADE IT TO A ROAD

SIDE PARK ABOUT 10 MILES OUTSIDE OF TOWN. WE DISCUSSED THE TIRE

AND BOTH AGREED IT WOULD LAST UNTIL JACK'S SISTERS HOUSE. THE

BUGS WERE BACK AND THE SPRAY WORKED ONCE AGAIN. THE WEATHER

FRONT HAD MISSED US TO THE SOUTH BUT WE DID GET WET A FEW TIMES

TODAY. WE SAT AND TALKED FOR AN HOUR OUR TWO ABOUT EVERYTHING

WE HAD SEEN AND DONE THE PAST 48 HOURS.

DAY 43 OF 53—SEPTEMBER 21ST, 1971—TUESDAY

WE GOT A VERY EARLY START BECAUSE OF THE TIRE AND MILES BEFORE

WE COULD FIX IT. IT MADE FOR ANOTHER DAY OF JUST KNOWING

SOMETHING WRONG WAS GOING TO HAPPEN, YOU JUST DIDN'T KNOW WHEN. WE PULLED INTO **"OCMULGEE NATIONAL MONUMENT"** NEAR MACON, GEORGIA AND METHODICALLY WENT THROUGH THE PRESENTATIONS WHEN MY MIND WAS ON THE TIRE. I EVEN FORGOT TO TAKE PICTURES OF THE SITE. I DO REMEMBER IT WAS SOMETHING TO DO WITH THE LOCAL NATIVE INDIANS AND THE WAY THEY LIVED.

AFTER A LOT OF MILES ON A POOR TIRE WE ARRIVED AT JACK'S SISTERS HOME IN ATLANTA, GEORGIA. WE DUMPED OUR GEAR OFF AND TOOK MY BIKE IN TO THE HONDA DEALER. AT 6 P.M. WE GOT IT BACK WITH A NEW TIRE FOR $25.46. THE DEALER THROUGH IN AN OIL CHANGE AND A TUNE UP. THAT WASN'T THE ONLY SURPRISE OF THE DAY. WHEN I GOT BACK TO THE HOUSE JACK WAS STANDING IN FRONT OF THE STOVE COOKING STEAKS. WE SPENT THE EVENING DISCUSSING THE TRIP.

DAY 44—SEPTEMBER 22ND, 1971—WEDNESDAY

BREAKFAST WAS BIG. JACK THEN HAD TO TUNE UP HIS BIKE AND WE BOTH WASHED THEM UP. WHEN THE KIDS CAME HOME WE TOOK OFF TO THE SITES AROUND TOWN. **"STONE MOUNTAIN"** WAS NOT COMPLETED YET BUT IT WAS CLEAR WHAT THE FINISHED PRODUCT WOULD LOOK LIKE. THE AREA AROUND THE MOUNTAIN HAD LOTS OF MUSEUM TYPE OF ARTIFACTS. A MOONSHINE STILL AND COVERED BRIDGE WERE TWO OF THE ATTRACTIONS.

DINNER THAT NIGHT WAS EXCEPTIONAL. JACKS SISTER WENT ALL OUT.

DAY 45—SEPTEMBER 23RD, 1971—THURSDAY

WE SAID GOODBYE TO JACKS RELATIVES AND THERE HOSPITALITY AND

IT WAS ON THE ROAD AGAIN.

OUR TARGET ON THE MAP WAS THE **<u>SMOKEY MOUNTAIN NATIONAL</u>**

<u>PARK</u>".

JACK AND I WERE BACK IN THE ELEMENTS. IT WAS THE MOUNTAINS AND

STREAMS RUNNING NEXT TO THE ROAD THAT GOT US BACK INTO THE

SADDLE SO TO SPEAK. WE HAD BEEN PAMPERED TOO MUCH AND IT WAS

TIME TO ROUGH IT AGAIN. THE OFF AND ON RAIN ALL MORNING AND MIST

FROM LOW CLOUDS ANSWERED THE CALL OF NATURE. WE STOPPED AT

LOTS OF ROADSIDE AREAS TO TAKE A BREAK AND JUST SOAK IN THE

SCENERY. SOMEWHERE AT THE TOP OF ONE OF THESE MOUNTAINS WE

LOOKED IN OUR REAR VIEW MIRRORS AND THERE WAS A GROUP OF HARLEYS CATCHING UP WITH US. THEY PASSED US BY LIKE WE WERE ON ROLLER SKATES. COMPARED TO THE HORSEPOWER THEY WERE ON THAT WASN'T A BAD COMPARISON. IT WAS THE HELLS ANGELS AGAIN. A DIFFERENT GROUP OF COURSE BUT WE DID THE SAME AS LAST TIME; LOTS OF DISTANCE BETWEEN US.

WE CAME DOWN THE MOUNTAIN AND INTO A SMALL TOWN CALLED GATLINBURG, TENNESSEE. IT WAS EVIDENT THE PEOPLE WERE 10 YEARS SLOW IN KEEPING UP WITH THE REST OF US SO WE GASED UP AND TRIED TO MAKE IT OUT WITHOUT ANY TROUBLE. WELL, "BUBBA", THE TOWNS OFFICER, PULLED US OVER AND SAID WE WERE BREAKING THE LAW. WE ASK WHICH LAW AND KNEW WE WERE IN TROUBLE WHEN HE TOOK SEVERAL MINUTES TO ANSWER. HE WALKED AROUND OUR BIKES AND REPLIED "TWO BIKES CANT RIDE SIDE BY SIDE IN THIS COUNTY". WE SAID WE DIDN'T KNOW THAT AND WE WERE JUST PASSING THROUGH. HE TOLD US HE WOULD BE WATCHING US AND WANTED US OUT OF HIS TOWN. NO PROBLEM—GOODBYE! WE WENT DOWN THE ROAD TO **"CHATTANOOGA BATTLEFIELD"** AND LEARNED MORE ABOUT THE CIVIL WAR. EACH ONE OF THESE STOPS HAS A STORY IN ITSELF BUT WE WOULD NEVER GET TO THE END OF THE TRIP.

AFTER A FEW MORE STOPS WE DECIDED WE NEEDED A BREAK AND PULLED INTO A COFFEE SHOP FOR SOME PEACAN PIE AND COFFEE. IT WAS GETTING COLD AGAIN AND WE KNEW WE NEEDED TO PICK A SPOT FOR THE

NIGHT. WE PULLED OFF INTO THE WOODS AND SACKED OUT. IT WASN'T BUT A HALF HOUR OR SO AFTER WE PASSED OUT WHEN A TRUCK WITH A LOAD OF PIGS PULLED OVER AND DECIDED TO STAY THE NIGHT. AT FIRST THE SOUND SCARED US BUT ONCE WE FIGURED IT OUT WE WENT BACK TO SLEEP.

DAY 46—SEPTEMBER 24TH, 1971—FRIDAY

THE DAY STARTED SLOW. IT MUST HAVE BEEN THE VERY LITTLE SLEEP I GOT DUE TO ONE EYE AND ONE EAR CONSTANTLY FOCUSING ON THE NOISE OF THE PIGS. LIKE JACK AND I THE TRUCKER GOT AN EARLY START. THE SUN WASN'T EVEN UP YET AND THE TRUCKER STARTED HIS MOTOR. 15 MINUTES LATER HE WAS PULLING OUT AND THE NOISE WENT QUICKLY TO A PEACEFUL CALM. I ENJOYED THE CALM FOR A FEW MINUTES AND THEN REACHED OVER AND GAVE JACK A TUG ON HIS SLEEPLING BAG. HE MUST HAVE BEEN DEAD TIRED THE NIGHT BEFORE BECAUSE HE SLEPT OKAY ALL NIGHT.

ONCE AGAIN THE DEW AND FOG WAS SO THICK YOU COULD CUT IT WITH A KNIFE. IT WAS A COLD MORNING AROUND 35—40 DEGREES. THE DEW ON SOME OF THE BRANCHES AND ROCKS HAD ICE ON THEM THAT HAD FORMED OVER THE NIGHT. I REMEMBER SLIPPING ON THE ROCKS AFTER I HAD MY BOOTS ON.

THE ONLY THING THAT WAS PUSHING ME THIS MORNING AND KEEPING ME FROM JUMPING BACK INTO THE SLEEPING BAG WAS MY MOTHER. YEP

NASHVILLE, TENNESSEE WAS JUST DOWN THE ROAD AND I KNEW

BREAKFAST WOULD BE WAITING.

THE RIDE INTO NASHVILLE WAS UNEVENTFUL, YET NICE. I SWEAR I

COULD SMELL MY MOTHERS COOKING FROM MILES OUT. AFTER ARRIVING

IT WASN'T 15 MINUTES AFTER SHE SAID "ARE YOU HUNGRY"? THEY TEACH

MOTHERS THAT! IT'S OUR JOBS TO ALWAYS SAY YES! I WAS NOW IN A

COMFORTABLE SETTING LIKE JACK WAS WITH HIS RELATIVES. WE SETTLED

INTO ANOTHER PAUSE IN OUR TRIP TO VISIT WITH RELATIVES. IT WAS

STEAKS AND BEER THAT EVENING WHEN MY SISTER AND FAMILY CAME BY

FOR ANOTHER ROUND OF FAMILY REUNION…BUT—THAT'S ANOTHER

STORY.

DAY 47—SEPTEMBER 25TH, 1971—SATURDAY

WE HAD EVERY INTENTION OF LEAVING THIS MORNING. LIKE ALL

MOTHERS, SHE STARTED IN ON ME AND WAS RELENTLESS. SHE INFORMED

ME OF THE DAY THAT SHE HAD SCHEDULED AND "NO" WAS NOT GOING TO

BE ACCEPTED. SHE TALKED ABOUT BEER, STEAKS, HORSESHOES, MORE

FAMILY COMING OVER…AND ON AND ON. JACK WAS OKAY WITH

EVERYTHING SO WE TWISTED EACH OTHERS ARMS AND LET EVERYONE

PAMPER US. AFTER THOUSANDS OF MILES ON THE ROAD IT DIDN'T TAKE

VERY MUCH TWISTING AT ALL.

YES, WE HAD OPPORTUNITY TO SEE THE TOWN AND BUILDINGS AND

SUCH…BUT THAT'S ANOTHER STORY.

DAY 48—SEPTEMBER 26TH, 1971—SUNDAY

I WASN'T ABOUT TO FALL INTO THE SAME TRAP TODAY FOR THE SIMPLE REASON THAT OUR NEXT STOP WAS JACKSON, MISSISSIPPI WHERE ONE OF MY OTHER SISTERS LIVED. MY MOTHER GAVE IT A GOOD EFFORT BY THE NICE BREAKFAST AND SAID IF WE STAYED WE WERE IN FOR A BIG SURPRISE FOR DINNER—BUT, THAT DIDN'T WORK.

AS WE GOT ONTO OUR BIKES THE WIND WAS KICKING UP AND THE SKY WAS VERY OVERCAST. IT WASN'T 10 MILES DOWN THE ROAD WE HIT RAIN. IT WAS COMING DOWN FROM ALL ANGLES. THE WIND WAS PUSHING US ALL OVER THE ROAD AND THE RAIN AND DARKNESS, DO TO THE HEAVY CLOUD COVER, WAS MAKING IT VERY DIFFICULT TO CONTINUE. IF WE WOULD NOT HAVE HAD A WARM BED AND MEAL AHEAD OF US IN JACKSON I WOULD HAVE TURNED BACK.

WE PULLED INTO **<u>SHILOH NATIONAL MILITARY PARK</u>** AROUND 9:30 A.M. AND WE WERE SOAKED. WE TOOK REFUGE AT THE VISITORS CENTER AND WELCOMED THE BREAK FROM THE ELEMENTS OUTSIDE. WE BOTH WISHED FOR A BETTER DAY BECAUSE OF THE AREA BUT YOU TAKE WHAT YOU GET. NO PICTURES WERE TAKEN JUST MEMORIES OF US LOOKING OUT OF THE VISITORS WINDOWS AT OUT BIKES STANDING IN RAIN THAT WAS NOW COMING DOWN IN BUCKETS. WE TOOK A LOOK AT EACH OTHER HOPING FOR ONE OF US TO HAVE AN ALTERNATIVE BUT THERE WASN'T ONE. WE PUT OUR HELMETS ON AND WALKED CASUALLY TOWARDS OUR

BIKES PASSING TOURIST WHO WERE RUNNING FRANTICALLY FOR COVER. THE LOOKS OF AMAZEMENT FROM THEM WERE ACCEPTED WITH A COMBINATION OF PRIDE FOR WHAT WE WERE DOING AND WHAT WE HAD TO GO THROUGH IN ORDER TO DO IT. IT ONLY TOOK A MINUTE BEFORE THE WATER WAS SEEPING INTO AREAS UNPROTECTED. THAT'S ACTUALLY A GOOD THING HOWEVER. YOU SEE YOU CAN THEN REARRANGE YOUR GEAR TO ACCOMMODATE THE OPENING AND GET ALL SITUATED FOR THE RIDE. IT'S DOWN RIGHT IMPOSSIBLE TO MAKE THOSE ADJUSTMENTS GOING DOWN THE ROAD AT 55 MPH. NOW COMPLETELY COVERED IN GEAR FROM HEAD TO TOE WE HEADED DOWN THE ROAD. THE **"NATCHEZ TRACE PARKWAY"** IS A BEAUTIFUL, NONE FREEWAY, ROAD THAT STRECHES FROM NATCHEZ, MISSISSIPPI TO NASHVILLE, TENNESSEE. IT WAS A COMPLETE SHAME THAT WE WERE PASSING THROUGH THIS AREA SQUINTING THROUGH THE DROUPLETS ON OUR FACESHIELDS WHILE FIGHTING THE DOWNPOUR OF RAIN. WE COULD TELL THIS PARKWAY IS A BIKERS ROAD. THE SLOW CURVES AND GENTLE HILLS WITH HEAVY VEGITATION ON BOTH SIDES. FOR MANY MILES WE DROVE WITH VIRTUALLY NO TRAFFIC AT ALL. I CAUGHT MYSELF IN A BEAUTIFUL RIDING MOOD. YOU HAVE TO RIDE TO UNDERSTAND THAT EVEN IN THIS WILD AND BIZARRE WEATHER, THE RIDE CAN BE MOST ENJOYABLE. ONCE YOU SETTLE IN AND FOCUS ON THE SURROUNDING AND ACCEPT THEM FOR WHAT THEY ARE AND DON'T FIGHT THEM; IT CAN BE MOST REWARDING. THE TRANCE I WAS IN WAS ENDED WHEN WE SAW THE SIGN TO JACKSON, MISSISSIPPI. PULLING OFF THE

PARKWAY ROAD AND HEADING TOWARDS JACKSON THE RAIN SEEMED TO
LIGHTEN UP A BIT. IT WAS NOW 4:30 OR SO AN WE MADE IT TO MY SISTERS
AROUND 6 P.M. AFTER STOPPING FOR FUEL. SHE HURRIED US IN OUT OF THE
RAIN AND WE TOOK SHOWERS AND SETTLED IN FOR A NIGHT OF VISITING.

DAY 49—SEPTEMBER 27TH, 1971—MONDAY

IT'S GREAT TO HAVE A LOT OF RELATIVES AND FRIENDS WHEN YOU
PLAN THESE TRIPS. WE WOKE UP TO ANOTHER FANTASTIC BREAKFAST AND
WE WERE NOW DRY AND IN A TOTALLY DIFFERENT SETTING THAN THE DAY
BEFORE.

WE TOOK THE OPPORTUNITY TO GO VISIT THE HONDA DEALER AND CHANGE OUR OIL, GREASE THE CHAIN, TIGHTEN UP BOLTS AND DO A GENERAL MAINTENANCE JOB ON THE BIKES. STILL NO MAJOR PROBLEMS WITH THE HONDA'S.

WE HEADED BACK TO MY SISTERS AND IT WAS MORE RELAXING TIME. AFTER DINNER JACK SACKED OUT AND I STAYED UP TALKING WITH HER ALL NIGHT. BUT…THAT'S ANOTHER STORY.

CHAPTER 11

DAY 50—SEPTEMBER 28TH, 1971—TUESDAY

ANOTHER WONDERFUL BREAKFAST AND A QUICK KISS ON MY SISTER

CHEEK AND AWAY WE WENT. THE SKY WAS ACTUALLY CLEAR—WOW!

THE **"VICKSBURG NATIONAL MILITARY PARK"** IS VERY

REPRESENTABLE TO MANY OF THE AREAS THAT EACH STATE HAS SHOWN

TRIBUTE TO THERE BATTLE AND WAR EFFORTS DURING THE CIVIL WAR. THE

PARK HAD SO MUCH TO TAKE IN THAT IT WAS HOURS BEFORE WE LEFT. WE

GOT CAUGHT UP IN THE OUTDOORS SINCE THE SUN WAS OUT AND

EVERYTHING WAS GREEN AND WELL MANICURED. WALKING AROUND THE

PARK WE STARTED FEELING HEAT FROM OUT LEATHERS FOR THE FIRST

TIME IN A LONG TIME. IT FELT GOOD.

JACK TOOK HIS LEATHER TOP OFF AND PUT A SHIRT ON AND I DID THE

SAME. WE GOT BACK ON OUR BIKES AND WAS REALLY FEELING GOOD. WE

CROSED OVER THE MISSISSIPPI RIVER AND GOT GAS AT TALLULAH,

LOUISIANA. WE HAD JUST DRIVEN INTO OUR 33rd STATE AND PASSED OVER COUNTLESS BRIDGES AND RIVERS, BUT, THE MISSISSIPPI RIVER IS ONE TO REMEMBER. TO ME, IT WASN'T BEAUTIFUL OR ANYTHING LIKE THAT. IT WAS MORE OF PUTTING A FACE TO A NAME TYPE OF EXPERIENCE. EVERYTHING THAT I HAD HEARD OR READ CAME RUSHING BACK INTO MY HEAD WHILE I WAS CROSSING HER.

WHEN WE GOT TO MONROE, LOUISIANA TO FILL UP WITH GAS IT WAS ONLY 4 P.M. OR SO BUT THE LAST FEW DAYS OF HOSPITALITY MADE US SOFT AND WE GOT ANOTHER ROOM. THERE IS NO OTHER WAY TO DISCRIBE IT, EXCEPT TO SAY WE FELT THE END OF OUR TRIP CLOSING DOWN ON US AND WE SORT OF WANTED TO DRAG IT OUT A LITTLE. A SIX PACK, A ROOM AND A CONVERSATION WITH THE LOCAL GIRLS AT THE HAMBURGER STAND ALSO PLAYED A PART IN THIS DELAY…BUT, THAT'S ANOTHER STORY.

DAY 51—SEPTEMBER 29TH, 1971—WEDNESDAY

WOW—WHAT A DIFFERENCE A NIGHT MAKES WHEN YOU SPEND IT WITH THE ONES YOU LOVE. THE MORNING AIR WAS FRESH, THE BIRDS WERE SINGING AND THE SKY WAS CLEAR. WE HEADED SOUTH TO THE GULF OF MEXICO. AT ALEXANDRIA, LOUISIANA WE TOOK 165 SOUTH AND STOPPED IN OAKDALE FOR GAS. COUNTING THE DOLLARS I HAD IN RESERVE AND NOTEING THE DAYS LEFT, I STARTED TO SPURGE. WE'RE TALKING CANDY BARS, SODAS, EVEN AN ORANGE. BACK ON THE BIKES WE WERE 5 YEARS YOUNGER. STILL WITHOUT OUR LEATHER TOPS AND NO FACESHIELDS WE

WERE CUTTING UP LIKE IT WAS OUR FIRST DAY ON THE TRIP. THE CLOSER

AND CLOSER WE CAME TO GULF THE WARMER IT GOT. WHEN WE GOT TO

THE COAST IT WAS EMPTY. MILES AND MILES OF NOTHING BUT BEACH.

HIGHWAY 87 FROM PORT ARTHUR TO GALVESTON WAS EMPTY. WE

ROAD FOR MILES AND SAW VERY FEW CARS. WE DECIDED TO STOP AND

STRETCH OUR LEGS ON THE BEACH AND JUST ENJOY THE SUN FOR A MINUTE

OR TWO. THE SEA GULLS WERE ENTERTAINING US WHEN WE MADE UP OUR

MINDS TO PUSH ON. AT THE END OF THIS STRETCH WE GOT ANOTHER TREAT.

IN ORDER TO GET TO GALVESTON, TEXAS FROM HIGHWAY 87 YOU MUST

TAKE THE "FREE" FERRY. YEP—THE TEXAS HIGHWAY DEPARTMENT PAYS

FOR YOUR TRIP. WE WERE FIXING TO ADD ANOTHER FIRST TO OUR TRIP.

DRIVING ONTO THE FERRY AND RELAXING TO THE SOUNDS AROUND US,

JACK AND I HAD A RARE OPPORTUNITY TO WATCH THE SCENERY GO BY

WITH A NEW PERSPECTIVE. THE DAY WAS TRULY TURNING INTO ONE OF

OUR BEST.

WE MADE IT INTO HOUSTON, TEXAS AROUND 5 P.M. AND STOPPED TO

TAKE A PICTURE OF THE ASTRODOME BEFORE FINDING ANOTHER FRIEND OF

MINE. THIS FRIEND HAD MARRIED OUR HIGHSCHOOL ENGLISH TEACHER

AND HE WAS NOW GOING TO RICE UNIVERSITY…BUT - THAT'S ANOTHER

STORY.

I HELPED HIM PUT HIS TRANSMISSION IN HIS CAR THAT EVENING AND

SHE COOKED FOR US AND GAVE US A PLACE TO SLEEP FOR THE NIGHT.

BEER AND STORIES OF HIGHSCHOOL TOOK US WELL INTO THE NIGHT

BEFORE WE GOT ANY SLEEP.

DAY 52—SEPTEMBER 30TH, 1971—THURSDAY

THEY BOTH LEFT EARLY FOR SCHOOL SO JACK AND I LOCKED UP AND

STARTED DOWN THE ROAD. WE MADE IT TO AUSTIN, TEXAS AROUND 9 A.M.

AFTER STOPPING FOR GAS IN COLUMBUS, TEXAS. THE ATTENDANT TOLD US

NOT TO MISS THE CAPITOL BUILDING IN AUSTIN. THIS WAS A DEPARTURE

FROM MY GOALS BUT THE TRIP WAS NEARING END SO ONE MORE CAPITOL

BUILDING WOULDN'T HURT. WHILE WE WERE PARKED AND GETTING

READY TO LEAVE A YOUNG CONGRESSMAN CAME OVER AND STARTED

TALKING WITH US AND BECAME VERY INTERESTED IN OUR TRIP.

SAN ANTONIO, TEXAS WAS JUST DOWN THE ROAD AND WE STOPPED AT

THE RIVER WALK DOWNTOWN AND HAD A BURGER. THE RIVER RUNS RIGHT

THROUGH DOWNTOWN AND THERE ARE LOTS OF SHOPS FOR THE TOURIST

TO BE ATTRACTED TO. THIS WASN'T WHAT WE WERE THERE FOR OF COURSE

BUT WE DID NEED A BREAK. THE **"ALAMO NATIONAL MONUMENT"** WAS

ALSO DOWNTOWN. THIS BUILDING WITH IT'S HISTORY MEANT A LOT TO ME

SINCE I WAS A TEXAN BY HEART. JACK AND I WERE INTERESTED IN THE

AREA BUT NOT IMPRESSED. I HAD EXPECTED EVEN MORE OF AN

ELABORATE DISPLAY. AND THE FACT THAT THIS FORT STOOD RIGHT DOWN

TOWN AMONG ALL THE OTHER HIGH RISES TOOK AWAY FROM IT'S

FRONTIERISM STIGMA. STILL, THE INFORMATION AVAILABLE THERE WAS

GOOD.

THE SUN WAS MAKING ITS WAY TOWARDS SUNSET SO WE HEADED OUT

OF TOWN. IT WAS LATE IN THE EVENING WHEN WE GOT TO JUNCTION,

TEXAS. THIS WOULD BE OUR LAST NIGHT CAMPING OUT AND ROUGHING IT

BESIDE THE ROADS AND DEALING WITH THE ELEMENTS. WE STOPPED AT

THE LOCAL GROCERIES STORE AND PICKED UP FOOD AND BEER AND

HEADED FOR WHAT I CALL THE PERFECT SPOT. THERE DIDN'T SEEM TO BE

ANYTHING SPECIAL ABOUT THE TOWN, JUST THAT WE WERE THERE. THE

SUN WAS SETTING AND THE LIGHTS WERE STARTING TO COME ON HERE

AND THERE AROUND TOWN. THE CAMPSITE THAT WE HAPPENED UPON OVERLOOKED THE VALLEY AND TOWN. AS JACK AND I GAZED OUT OVER THE SCENERY WE COULDN'T HELP BUT REFLECT THE DAYS PAST. OUR CONVERSATION WAS DIFFERENT TONIGHT; WE PICKED OUR FAVORITE SITES, REMEMBERED THE ANTS, BEES, BUGS, SUNSETS AND SUNRISES. AS INCREDIBLE OF A TRIP WE HAD MADE, ENDURING HARDSHIPS AND WITNESSING FEELINGS WE NEVER NEW WE HAD, WE DID NOT WANT IT TO END. THIS IS WHY I KEEP THIS PICTURE CLOSE TO MY HEART.

AS THE DAY TURNED TO NIGHT JACK AND I CONTINUED TALKING ABOUT THE TRIP. TWO SIX PACKS LATER, IT WAS PITCH DARK AND THE TEXAS SKY HAD OPENED UP TO REVEAL HER BEAUTY. THE STARS WERE IN THE

BILLIONS AND EACH WERE SHARPLY DEFINED BECAUSE THE SMALL TOWNS

LIGHTS COULD NOT COMPETE. THE ONLY COMPETITION WAS THE MANY

SNAPSHOTS IN OUR MINDS OF VARIOUS MOMENTS AND PLACES WE HAD

BEEN. YET, COMPARING OUR TRIP TO THE NIGHT SKY WE HAD ONLY

VISITED A FEW OF THE MANY STARS. BOTH OF US KNEW WE HAD ONLY

SCRATCHED THE SURFACE OF WHAT WAS AVAILABLE TO TRAVELERS IN

AMERICA. WE WOULD CONTINUE OUR TRIP TOMORROW VISITING ONE OR

TWO MORE UNBELIEVABLE SITES KNOWING THAT TONIGHT WAS OUR LAST

UNDER THE STARS. THERE WAS NO RAIN, WIND, BUGS OR NOISE TO DISTURB

THIS MOMENT, ONLY JACK AND I AND OUR BIKES!

DAY 53—OCTOBER 1ST, 1971—FRIDAY

DURING THE NIGHT IT RAINED SEVERAL TIMES BUT ONLY SHORT CLOUD BURST. THE AIR WAS CRYSTAL CLEAR AND ONLY A FEW CLOUDS WERE OFF TO THE NORTHEAST OF US. WE WERE NOW HEADING NORTHWEST. A MORNING RIDE BETWEEN GAS STATIONS GOT US TO FT. STOCKTON, TEXAS AROUND 10 A.M. WE TURNED NORTH ON 285 AND FOLLOWED THE PECOS RIVER FOR HOURS. JACK TOOK LOTS OF PICTURES OF THE DESERT BEFORE OUR NEXT STOP AT **"CARLSBAD CAVERNS NATIONAL PARK".** THIS HOLE IN THE GROUND, AS JACK DESCRIBED IT, WAS A SPECTACULAR SITE THAT I HAD VISITED SEVERAL TIMES AS A KID. WE WERE NOW ONLY HOURS AWAY FROM EL PASO, TEXAS. MY PICTURES DID NOT TURN OUT GOOD ENOUGH TO MAKE THIS BOOK BUT THE TOTAL I TOOK SHOULD SAY IT BY ITSELF (12 SHOTS). THIS IS A SPOT YOU DON'T WANT TO MISS. ON THE WAY TO EL PASO WE PASSED THROUGH BUT DID NOT STOP IN **"GUADALUPE MOUNTAINS NATIONAL PARK".** FOR THE LOCALS THIS PARK IS BEAUTIFUL AND A LOT OF SCENIC SPOTS BUT WE HAD GONE THROUGH THE BEST AND IT JUST COULD NOT COMPARE.

WHEN WE PULLED INTO EL PASO IT WAS LATE BUT WE JUST HAD TO HAVE A PICTURE OF "THE END OF THE TRAIL". SO WE OPENED THE GARAGE, TURNED ON THE LIGHTS AND HAD MY LANDLADY TAKE THE FINAL SHOT; <u>THE TRADITIONAL HANDSHAKE</u>. IT WAS OUT OF FOCUS AND OUR HEADS WERE CHOPPED OFF BUT SHE GOT THE HAND SHAKE.

DAYS—53

MILES—15,828

COST—$334.22

<u>*CHAPTER 12*</u>

"THE END" - JUST IS NOT APPROPRIATE! MANY HOURS, DAYS AND YEARS WENT INTO THIS TRIP. I CAN ALMOST TRACE BACK MY WHOLE CHILDHOOD THROUGH EVENTS THAT ADDED ANOTHER STOP, OR ANOTHER FRIEND TO THE LIST. EACH AND EVERY DAY OF OUR LIVES, MOLDS THE REST OF OUR LIFE FOR US. SINCE THE SERVICE, AND AFTER THIS BIKE TRIP I GRADUATED FROM UNIVERSITY OF TEXAS AT EL PASO WITH A BUSINESS DEGREE, BECAME COMPTROLLER FOR A LARGE COMPANY, WENT ON TO BECOME DATA PROCESSING MANAGER, THEN BRANCH MANAGER, THEN SALES MANAGER AND ON AND ON.

ALL OF THESE ACCOMPLISHMENTS STARTED WHEN A LITTLE BOY FOUND OUT HOW TO SET A GOAL, AND STAY WITH IT. I WANT TO THANK EVERYONE WHO HELPED AND ASSISTED IN THE TRIP. I ESPECIALLY WANT TO THANK JACK.

AND TO MY WIFE OF 30 YEARS - - **I'M READY TO DO IT AGAIN!!**

THE FOLLOWING PAGES SHOW ITEMS OF THE TRIP

SAMPLE OF MAPS

El Pasoan Takes 53-Day Vacation on Motorcycle

By BOB DONALDSON

A 15,000 mile trip across America became a reality for an El Pasoan and a friend when the two finished the 53 day motorcycle trek in El Paso.

Richard Ives, 21, of 5037 Vulcan avenue said that he has always wanted to travel, but for one reason or another had not been able to do so.

"When I was 15 I was determined to take a trip across the nation, and it was only this past August that I was able to do what I had planned," he said.

WHILE SERVING with the Army at Ft. Carson, Colo., Richard met Jack Cramer, 21, of Fond du Lac, Wisc. who also shared the same desire to travel. Jack was discharged in January of this year and returned home to Wisconsin where he saved up enough money to buy a motorcycle and pay for expenses.

"On Aug. 10 I was discharged from Carson," Richard said. Jack was waiting at the gate. I had a detailed, eight page intinerary for the trip that I had planned long before I went into the Army, and we started."

Richard said that the main purpose behind the trip was to see America through its National Parks and historic sites. The travelers estimate that they saw 75 per cent of them.

"**MY COST** for the 53 days was $334.22, and that was for gas, oil and food. Otherwise we roughed it. Both of us had identical cycles, an all purpose mess kit, sleeping bag and our Army boots. We also had a pack for food," Richard said.

The two were stopped only once in their 15,826 mile journey and that was in New York.

"We were on a back road and a police car pulled us over," Richard said. "All he wanted to do was to check to see if the cycles were registered to us. There had been some stolen in the area. We were never stopped because of our leather outfits or later in the trip when our hair got long.

"**WE DIDN'T** shave or get a hair cut once during the trip, and it was just a time to do what we wanted."

When asked if the trip was valuable to them, Richard said, "I think my attitude toward America changed in the 53 days, I had been in the ... and had heard gripes from guys from all over the country on how bad the country was. Not just the people, but the land and their home states as well. After seeing 31 of the 48 adjacent states, I still say that America is one of the most beautiful places I've seen. This holds true especially in the National Parks. I hope to write a book about what we saw and did."

EL PASO, TEXAS NEWSPAPER

Cycling Through America

By SUSAN JULKA
(Feature Editor)

FROM LOOKING Glass Rock to Socorro and White Sands, from Las Vegas to Joshua Tree, N.M. and Yosemite. From one end of the country to the other, two young men roar on Honda 175s in what will amount to an estimated 20,000 mile journey of America.

"We wanted to see America while we can, not that the countryside won't be there tomorrow, but we may never have the opportunity again," explained 21-year-old Richard Ives of Texas, who with Jack Kramer, city, is touring the country, El Paso to El Paso.

Jack, also 21, the son of Mr. and Mrs. Victor Kramer, 236 E. 14th St., met Richard while both were serving with the U.S. Army's 5th Division Honor Guard at Ft. Carson, Colo. Between military parades and funerals, the two planned the trip that had been Richard's dream since age 15 and his first motorcycle.

Sitting around the barracks, the two planned the 20,000 mile trip to historical sites, national parks and monuments, using chiefly a Texaco Travel Guide to plan their route.

A Memory of America

On Aug. 10, six weeks after his 21st birthday and the purchase of the new cycle, Jack set out from Fond du Lac for Colorado Springs, Colo., where he met Richard and the ride began. Richard, newly mustered out of the service, had bought the same size bike and the two hit the road.

For a month, they drove the sideroads and byways of the United States, seeing its most historic points and its most beautiful ones. Richard stated, "We hoped to visit various parts of the U.S. and record her beauty in our memories."

Each man wears leather pants and shirt for protection from falls and weather and with them on the bikes, tied to the sissy bars, is their gear: C rations, sandwiches, a black log book where the trip is charted and expenses are noted, a can opener, Army mess kit, camera, toilet articles and four changes of underwear and socks.

Their trip is planned to the last mile, the last park, the last relative or friend to visit on the way. Having completed the western segment of their journey, the two were in Fond du Lac over Labor Day weekend for a brief rest and laundry stop at the Kramers. When they left early Wednesday for Chicago and points East, they carried sandwiches Mrs. Kramer had prepared for their trip.

Dirt Means Irritability

The Eastern portion of their trip will cover Niagara Falls, Baxter State Park in Maine and historic sites in Washington, D.C., Pennsylvania and Virginia. From there, they'll take the Eastern coast through Virginia, Georgia and Florida, all the way down to the Key West Islands, then up to Tennessee and back to Texas.

Twenty thousand miles is a long way to travel by motorcycle or any other way and the cyclists' main complaint is dirt: "After about three days of riding and no shower, we get pretty irritable. We see things we'd appreciate a lot more if we were clean. Then we hit a place to shower, and things look better again."

Things they've learned on the road include the fact that Wisconsin has more bugs than any other state, forcing the riders to wear their face shields. Washington and Oregon thus far have had the best-marked roads. California has no helmet law. And it only costs $10 for a Golden Eagle Passport to the nation's parks. So far, Jack and Richard have each visited $21 worth of parks on that passport.

Asked if they are hassled by natives of the states they visit or park rangers, Richard, in his strong Texas drawl, was quick to reply, "People sure do look, but we soon meet them and everyone's real nice. They tell us what sites not to miss and are real helpful."

Less Than a Cent a Mile

They ride stock bikes, sleep at waysides and restspots and will spend a total of $350 each, for food and gas. On a Honda, it costs less than a cent a mile to see America.

Showers are taken at every available spot and the most interesting one was enjoyed in a reservoir and irrigation ditch, standing on a cement runway under an outlet eight feet above their heads. "We take some weird showers," Jack noted.

Richard says he met Jack at just the right time, allowing a lifetime dream trip to come true. They estimate that the trip will take a total of two months, months they can spare at 21 but that will probably never be available again.

They travel 400 miles a day and have had no problems more serious than a broken chain. They've driven Death Valley, the oceanside roadways of America and sped through the giant redwoods of California. They've seen the Grand Teutons, Yelowstone and Utah's Arches National Monument.

Two months of recording America's beauty in their memories, two months of living on the open road, two months of easy riding.

FOND du LAC, WISCONSIN NEWSPAPER

THE HANCOCK BUILDING in Chicago is the next spot to see for Richard Ives of El Paso, Tex., left, and Jack Kramer, city, who are making a 20,000 mile tour of America by motorcycle. Their trip began when Jack left Fond du Lac Aug. 10 and will last approximately two months. (Commonwealth Reporter Photo by Spike Knuth)

<u>BIKE TRIP OF THE UNITED STATES</u>

Richard Ives   Jack Kramer

<u>APPOXIMATELY</u> !?

Total Days -   -   -   -   75 Days

C.S to E.P. -   -   -   -   5 Days

E.P. to E.P. -   -   -   -   70 Days

Total Miles -   -   - -15000 Miles

Cost of Gas -   -   - $50.00

COST of Food   -   - $150.00

Depart   -   -   -   - 11 Aug. '71

Purpose: We hope to visite various parts of the US and
          record her beauty in our memories.

```
            ITEMS NEEDED ON BIKE TRIP


 1. Cycle- Honda, CL 350----------------------------------- 1
 2.Helmet, Safty------------------------------------------- 1
 3. Sissy Bar--------------------------------------------- 1
 4. Sleeping Bag, Artic----------------------------------- 1
 5. Water Proof Cover for Sleeping Bag-------------------- 1
 6. Blanket, Wool----------------------------------------- 1
 7. Gloves------------------------------------------------ 1 Pair
 8. Boots------------------------------------------------- 1 Pair
 9. Leather Suit------------------------------- 1 shirt,1 pants
10.Jacket, Field------------------------------------------ 1
11.Socks, Shorts and T-Shirts---------------------------- 4 Pair
12.Electric Razor- Rechargable Type---------------------- 1
13.ToothBrush with Paste--------------------------------- 1-1
14.Comb with Hair Dressing------------------------------- 1-1
15.Soap, Bar with Deodorant------------------------------ 1-1
16.Can Opener-------------------------------------------- 1
17.Matches, Box or Lighter------------------------------- 1
18.Mess "it- Army, Complete ----------------------------- 1
19.Shoe Polish, Black------------------------------------ 1
20.Shoe Brush ------------------------------------------- 1
21.Camera----------------------------------------------- 1
22.Film/Four Packs at all times(slides)----------------- 4
23. Pen and Pad Book------------------------------------ 1-1
```

LIST OF ITEMS FOR THE TRIP

<u>*ABOUT THE AUTHOR*</u>

BORN IN KENTUCKY; RAISED IN TEXAS. I MET ALL MY EDUCATION REQUIREMENTS WITH LITTLE ENTHUSIASM. I WAS DRAFTED INTO THE ARMY DURING THE VIETNAM ERA AND WAS PROUD TO WEAR THE UNIFORM THAT MY FATHER MADE A CAREER OF. AFTER MY MOTORCYCLE TRIP I MARRIED MY HIGH SCHOOL SWEETHEART AND THEN FINISHED COLLEGE AT UTEP. I THEN WENT ON TO A BUSINESS CAREER IN THE CONSTRUCTION EQUIPMENT INDUSTRY. I'VE HAD MY UPS AND DOWNS LIKE ANYONE, BUT I'VE ALWAYS TURNED TO MY BIKE TO WIND DOWN. IT'S A FEELING THAT ONLY A BIKER KNOWS AND I WISH IT FOR EVERYONE. I AM FORTUNATE TO HAVE MORE GOOD MEMORIES THAN BAD ONES AND WHEN THE BAD ONES COME UP I ALWAYS SHUT MY EYES AND REFLECT ON SOME PART OF MY TRIP.